PINK BEAMS FROM THE GOD IN THE GUTTER

The Science-Fictional Religion of Philip K. Dick

Gabriel Mckee

University Press of America,® Inc.
Dallas · Lanham · Boulder · New York · Oxford

Copyright © 2004 by
University Press of America,® Inc.
4501 Forbes Boulevard
Suite 200
Lanham, Maryland 20706
UPA Acquisitions Department (301) 459-3366

PO Box 317
Oxford
OX2 9RU, UK

All rights reserved
Printed in the United States of America
British Library Cataloging in Publication Information Available

Library of Congress Control Number: 2003111462
ISBN 0-7618-2673-4 (paperback : alk. ppr.)

∞™ The paper used in this publication meets the minimum
requirements of American National Standard for Information
Sciences—Permanence of Paper for Printed Library Materials,
ANSI Z39.48—1984

Contents

PREFACE On Religion and Science-Fiction   v

ACKNOWLEDGEMENTS   xi

CHAPTER ONE Anamnesis, 1 Corinthians, and Rocket Ships: Philip K. Dick as Religious Philosopher   1

CHAPTER 2 "A Scanner Darkly": Dick as a Christian Theologian   23

CHAPTER 3 Infinity, Play Again: The Nature and Importance of Dick's Religious Speculations   45

APPENDIX Biographical Notes on Philip K. Dick   73

WORKS CITED   77

INDEX   83

PREFACE

On Religion and Science-Fiction

In *Metamorphoses of Science Fiction*, his primary work on the nature of the genre of SF,[1] Prof. Darko Suvin argues against the incorporation of religious themes in science fiction, claiming they are antithetical to the genre itself. "All attempts," he claims, "to transplant the metaphysical orientation of mythology and religion into SF . . . will result only in private pseudomyths, in fragmentary fantasies or fairy tales."[2] Elsewhere, he states that "It is intrinsically or by definition impossible for SF to acknowledge any metaphysical agency, in the literal sense of an agency going beyond *physis* (nature). Whenever it does so, it is not SF, but a metaphysical or (to translate the Greek into Latin) a supernatural fairy-tale."[3] Suvin argues that "science fiction" must be rooted, first and foremost, in *science*, which by Suvin's definition does not and cannot admit or accept the metaphysical. Any science fiction that attempts to explore metaphysical issues, Suvin argues, ceases by that exploration to be science fiction. By his definition, SF is distinguished from naturalistic fiction "by the narrative dominance or hegemony of a fictional 'novum' (novelty, innovation) validated by cognitive logic."[4] The SF author's primary goal should be the creation of plausible—that is to say, scientific-materialist—worlds.

Not all writers and fans of SF assume those letters to stand for "science fiction," however. Another term for the genre has become popular in the

---

[1] Throughout this book, I will use the abbreviation "SF" for "science" or "speculative fiction." In addition to being the standard nomenclature in the field of SF criticism, this abbreviation preserves a certain ambiguity about the nature of the genre it describes. This ambiguity is necessary for my discussion of Dick's not-so-scientific SF.

[2] Darko Suvin, *Metamorphoses of Science Fiction: On the Poetics and History of a Literary Genre*. New Haven and London: Yale University Press, 1979, 26.

[3] Suvin, *Metamorphoses*, 66.

[4] Suvin, *Metamorphoses*, 63, italics removed.

last few decades, particularly among the authors themselves—"speculative fiction." This term morphologically broadens the variety of subject matter acceptable within the genre: not just scientific theorizing, but *any* form of speculation, is acceptable in SF. This term also has its problems, as any term that attempts to describe so large a body of literature must. But it nonetheless reveals the real purpose of SF—not simply to give us new scientific or cognitive ideas (Suvin's "novum"), but to give us new worlds to encounter and experience. Tom Woodman writes that what fascinates the reader of SF is generally not "the rockets that transport us to strange new worlds but the new worlds themselves."[5] Technology and science are in many ways tangential to SF, a means to an end. Its true goal is to explore humankind's quest for meaning as we are brought into the future and toward the stars.

Religion and SF, then, can be said to share many goals. Author Samuel R. Delany once wrote that "No matter how disciplined its creation, to move into an unreal world demands a brush with mysticism. Virtually all the classics of speculative fiction are mystical."[6] Most (though by no means all) SF deals with the future, which is by its very nature a "new world," different from that in which we live. The future, like the divine, is unknown and, in the present, unknowable. In Philip José Farmer's novel *To Your Scattered Bodies Go* a character gives the reason for exploration: "I will tell you that we are setting sail because the Unknown exists and we would make it Known."[7] SF concerns itself with the question of what new worlds we are moving towards. But more importantly, it asks the further question: When we arrive in this world, how shall we encounter it? How will it change us, and how will we change it? David Ketterer, acknowledging the importance of the future's new world in SF, sees it as a type of apocalyptic literature. He defines this as writing "concerned with the creation of other worlds which exist, on the literal level, in a credible relationship. . . with the 'real' world, thereby causing a metaphorical destruction of that 'real' world in the reader's head."[8]

---

[5] Tom Woodman, "Science fiction, religion and transcendence." In Patrick Parrinder, ed., *Science Fiction: A Critical Guide.* London: Longman Group, 1979, 121.

[6] Samuel R. Delany, "About Five Thousand One Hundred and Seventy Five Words." *Extrapolation* 10 (1969), 64.

[7] Philip José Farmer, *To Your Scattered Bodies Go.* New York: Berkely Medallion, 1971, 98 (§13).

[8] David Ketterer, *New Worlds for Old: The Apocalyptic Imagination, Science Fiction, and American Literature.* Bloomington, Indiana: Indiana University Press, 1974, 13.

ON RELIGION AND SCIENCE-FICTION

The template for SF, according to Ketterer, is not to be found in the writing of H. G. Wells, Edgar Allen Poe, or Jules Verne, but rather in the Book of Revelations, the archetype of literature in which a new world replaces an old one. Ketterer's understanding of the term "apocalyptic literature" is very different from the understanding of the term as it is used in the field of religious studies, and SF is not apocalyptic in this more narrow, technical sense. But Ketterer's argument is nonetheless compelling: *change* is the fundamental subject of SF. In a rapidly-changing world, we need solutions to the problems of tomorrow before they actually arrive; SF, though it cannot provide definitive answers, can at least attempt to predict what problems we may encounter, be they technological or theological.

This book is not about science fiction. It is about the theology—or more accurately, the theologies—discussed and explored by an author of science fiction, and though it draws on many of that author's works of fiction in exploring that theology, it focuses primarily on his religious nonfiction. As Ketterer and others have emphasized, science fiction can be—perhaps even *must* be—religious (if we may take, as a brief and partial definition of that term, a preoccupation with questions of ultimate meaning). SF has always been concerned with humankind's role in the expanding universe, and the purpose of that universe itself; these questions are arguably also at the basis of all religious thought. SF, then, can be religious, but the question that the religious speculations of Philip K. Dick raise is rather: Can religion be "science fictional"? SF writer Thomas M. Disch, in his history of the genre, claims that it can, and cites four main examples: L. Ron Hubbard's Church of Scientology, the Aum Shinrikyo cult, the Heaven's Gate community, and Philip K. Dick.[9] Does Dick fit in this category? Disch is adamant in his criticisms of the three larger communities of "SF religions," viewing them as manipulative cons at best and gatherings of genocidal lunatics at worst. He acknowledges Dick's difference from the three groups, but insists that he would have become just like them if he had only lived a few years longer. Disch claims that Dick experienced "the temptation, which had always been present but which must have grown greater after the publication of *Valis*, to parlay the muddy revelations of the *Exegesis* into official doctrine and

---

[9] Thomas M. Disch, *The Dreams our Stuff is Made of: How Science Fiction Conquered the World.* New York: The Free Press, 1998, 137-162 (Chapter 7, "When You Wish Upon a Star: Science Fiction as a Religion").

a church."[10] Dick's friend and fellow SF author Norman Spinrad similarly claims that some "have constructed a cult around the Divine Revelation of the Pink Light."[11] For these two authors, as well as many others, any infusion of science-fictional ideas into a religious framework can only lead to a lunatic cult. SF authors who think seriously about religious topics, or worse yet claim to have had religious experiences, are con men and pathological liars.

Despite the claims and accusations of these two authors, both of whom Dick counted among his friends, there is little in Dick's writings to imply he had any intention of starting a religious community of his own. He told others of his experiences, but these discussions were hardly attempts at proselytizing. Rather, they were a part of his personal process of understanding his experience, dialogues that helped to direct his ever-shifting theology and introduced new perspectives to that process. Perhaps it is because Disch and Spinrad were Dick's friends that they are so convinced that he was a potential cult-leader: they observed only that small part of Dick's theorizing that they witnessed personally, rather than seeing the entire process of theorizing and theologizing that preoccupied him for the last eight years of his life. Perhaps they fail to see a division between the sociological aspects of religion and its philosophical, theological, and personal aspects, seeing any form of religious speculation as a sign of the beginnings of a movement or a community. Regardless of why Disch and Spinrad view Dick's religious thought in such a negative light, their opinions reveal the overall conclusion of many SF fans and writers: SF and religion are ultimately incompatible, and any theology such a combination produces is likely to be a parody of "authentic" religion.

Examining Dick's religious writings themselves reveals another approach to the question of science-fictional religion, one that does not rely on SF theology devolving into what Spinrad calls "cultish rubbish."[12] Dick's religious writing deals first and foremost with theological and metaphysical themes, though it often does so in the terms of futurological fiction. Much of what he called his "*Exegesis*" consists of religious interpretations of works of SF, mostly his own. Further, a number of his theories regarding the source

---

[10] Disch, *The Dreams our Stuff is Made of,* 158.
[11] Norman Spinrad, *Science Fiction in the Real World.* Carbondale, Illinois: Southern Illinois University Press, 1990, 213.
[12] Spinrad, *Science Fiction in the Real World,* 198.

of his experiences involve extraterrestrials, ancient alien satellites, time travel, and energy beings. But this does not automatically place Dick in the category of Hubbard and the Heaven's Gate community: these theories, though essential to understanding Dick's religious thought, are still not the religious center of Dick's thought, nor are they the primary science-fictional element in his speculations. As stated above, the one goal of SF is to propose a wide variety of potential problems as well as possible solutions. Dick's religious writing, as will be discussed in more detail below, consists of repeated attempts to give as many possible theories explaining his religious experience as possible—to *speculate* on the meaning not only of his own encounters with what may have been the divine, but on the meaning of the universe as well. If SF is "speculative fiction," then in Dick we have a "speculative theology" that concerns itself not with God's actualities, but rather his possibilities and potentialities. It is science-fictional religion but not "cultish;" speculative but not random; radical but not ineffectual. Dick's writings pose religious questions to the human beings of the future; in this, they blend religion and SF in a truly original and vibrant way.

ACKNOWLEDGEMENTS

I would like to thank Professor Alan Hodder and Professor Robert Meagher for their help and guidance throughout the process of writing this paper, Professor Alec Irwin at Amherst College for his interest in the subject, Tom Dillingham for his help with my research, the entire Philip K. Dick mailing list for their help and support, my parents, Richard and Kathleen McKee, for funding my education (among countless other things), my friends for not letting my work come between us, Gwynne Watkins for the *caritas* I needed to finish the project, and Christine Fernsebner Eslao for typesetting the book and especially for lending me an old copy of *VALIS* three years ago: it was the clay pot in which lived God.

All material by Philip K. Dick reprinted by permission of the Philip K. Dick Testamentary Trust and its agents, Scovil Chichak Galen Literary Agency, Inc. Grateful acknowledgment is given for permission to use excerpts from *Philip K. Dick: The Dream Connection*, Copyright ©1999 D. Scott Apel. Reprinted by permission of the Impermanent Press (www.impermanentpress.com). Excerpts from *Augustine of Hippo: Selected Writings*, from The Classics of Western Spirituality Series, translated by Mary T. Clark, Copyright ©1984 by Mary T. Clark, Paulist Press, Inc., New York/Mahwah, NJ. Used with permission of Paulist Press (www.paulistpress.com). Grateful acknowledgement is given for permission to use excerpts from *The Philip K. Dick Society Newsletter*, Copyright ©1982-1987 Paul Williams, and *Only Apparently Real: The World of Philip K. Dick*, Copyright ©1986 Paul Williams. Reprinted by permission of Paul Williams. Grateful acknowledgement is given for permission to use excerpts from "Philip K. Dick on Philosophy: A Brief Interview" (*Niekas* No. 36, 1988) © 1986 Frank C. Bertrand. Originally published as "Philip K. Dick et la Philosophie: Une Courte Interview," trans. Sylvie Laine (*Yellow Submarine* No. 41, September 1986). Reprinted by permission of Frank C. Bertrand. Grateful acknowledgement is given for permission to use excerpts from *Divine Invasions: A Life of Philip K. Dick* and "On the Exegesis of Philip K. Dick," © 1999 and 1991 Lawrence Sutin. Reprinted by permission of Lawrence Sutin. Grateful acknowledgement is given for permission to use excerpts from *Philip K. Dick: In His Own Words* and *Philip K. Dick: The Last Testament,* © 1984 and 1985 Gregg Rickman. Reprinted by permission of Fragments West. Grateful acknowledgement is given for permission to use excerpts from *What If Our World Is Their Heaven? The Final Conversations of Philip K. Dick,* © 2000 Gwen Lee and Elaine Sauter. Reprinted by permission of the Overlook Press.

CHAPTER ONE

Anamnesis, 1 Corinthians, and Rocket Ships: Philip K. Dick as Religious Philosopher

> *I mean, after all; you have to consider we're only made out of dust. That's admittedly not much to go on and we shouldn't forget that. But even considering, I mean it's sort of a bad beginning, we're not doing too bad. So I personally have faith that even in this lousy situation we're faced with we can make it. You get me?*
> —Epigraph to *The Three Stigmata of Palmer Eldritch*, 1964

> *I've been doing these notes for this non-existent novel that will never get written. I've been warned by the publishers not to do any more philosophy stuff, so that's all over.*
> —Philip K. Dick in interview, 1981[1]

> *St. Paul said, "If I have not love then I am jack shit"... or something like that.*
> —Philip K. Dick in interview, 1977[2]

ZAPPED BY GOD: PHILIP K. DICK'S RELIGIOUS EXPERIENCE

In February 1974, a husky, bearded science-fiction writer named Philip K. Dick saw God, and he spent the rest of his life trying to figure out what it meant. Having sold his first short story in 1951, he had just published his 28th novel—*Flow My Tears, the Policeman Said*—and had just fathered his third child, the only son of his fifth and final marriage. Late in the February

---

[1] Gregg Rickman. *Philip K. Dick: The Last Testament.* Long Beach, California: Fragments West/Valentine Press, 1985, 1.
[2] D. Scott Apel. *Philip K. Dick: The Dream Connection, Second Edition.* San Jose, California: The Impermanent Press, 1999, 27.

of 1974, Dick had two impacted wisdom teeth removed under sodium pentathol. He describes the events that followed in a 1977 letter:

> Later that day we had to phone the pharmacy for some medication to ease the pain. I answered the knock on the door and found myself facing a young woman wearing around her neck a flashing necklace within the center of which a lovely golden fish was suspended. Fascinated, I kept staring at the golden fish, oblivious to the little bag of medication which she carried. "What is that fish for?" I asked her. Touching the golden fish, she answered, "It's a sign worn by the early Christians." Instantly a flash of something on the order of memory, but also on the order of understanding and belief, overcame me. I comprehended another world from the one I saw. All at once the reality of California 1974 was erased and an older reality replaced it—just for an instant.[3]

Dick expands on this account in a 1978 essay, stating that he had

> experienced what I later learned is called *anamnesis*—a Greek word meaning, literally, "loss of forgetfulness." I remembered who I was and where I was. In an instant, in the twinkling of an eye, it all came back to me. And not only could I remember it but I could see it. The girl was a secret Christian and so was I. We lived in fear of detection by the Romans. We had to communicate with cryptic signs. She had just told me all this, and it was true.
>   For a short time, as hard as this is to believe or explain, I saw fading into view the black, prisonlike contours of hateful Rome. But, of much more importance, I remembered Jesus, who had just recently been with us, and had gone temporarily away, and would very soon return. My emotion was one of joy. We were secretly preparing to welcome Him back. It would not be long. And the Romans did not know. They thought He was dead, forever dead. That was our great secret, our joyous knowledge. Despite all appearances, Christ was going to return, and our delight and anticipation were boundless.[4]

Dick's experience of living in apostolic times—"the world of *Acts*," as he would later describe it—was only the beginning of his religious experience.

---

[3] Philip K. Dick. *The Selected Letters of Philip K. Dick, Volume 5: 1977-1979*. Don Herron, ed. Novata, California: Underwood-Miller, 1993, 93.

[4] Philip K. Dick. "How to Build a Universe That Doesn't Fall Apart Two Days Later (1978)." In *The Shifting Realities of Philip K. Dick: Selected Literary and Philosophical Writings*, ed. Lawrence Sutin. New York: Vintage/Random House, 1995, 271.

He came to call this series of possibly mystical encounters "2-3-74," so named because they were most intense in February and March of 1974, though they continued intermittently until his death in 1982.

There was far more to Dick's experiences than the feeling that he was living in first-century Rome. Dick felt that he was being taken over by another personality—in a 1975 interview, Dick describes this as "the invasion of my mind by a transcendently rational mind, as if I had been insane all my life and suddenly had become sane."[5] He was never sure who this second personality really was—he theorized that it was a second-century Christian named Thomas, a form of living information which he called "Firebright," or the spirit of his friend, Episcopalian Bishop James A. Pike, who had died several years before in Israel. Regardless of the source of this second personality, Dick changed: he lost weight, fired his literary agent, and began drinking beer instead of wine, all for reasons unclear to him at the time.[6]

Dick also had a number of visionary experiences, in both waking and sleeping states. He referred to one of these as "St. Elmo's Fire," and a character's experience of it is described vividly in his novel *The Divine Invasion*, written in 1977:

> He looked around him and saw bamboo. But color moved through it, like St. Elmo's Fire. The color, a shiny, glistening red, seemed alive. It collected here and there, and where it gathered it formed words, or rather something like words. As if the world had become language... The fire moved; it came and it passed on; it flowed this way and that; pools of it formed, and he knew he was seeing a living creature. Or rather the *blood* of a living creature. The fire was living blood, but a magical blood, not physical blood but blood transformed.[7]

Dick believed that "St. Elmo's Fire" was both a form of living information and a glimpse of Absolute Reality—though he never settled on an answer about the actual nature of that reality. One visual experience that occupied much of his later theorizing on 2-3-74 involved seeing what he believed to be a tremendous number of abstract paintings, which he describes in a

---

[5] Charles Platt. *Dream Makers: The Uncommon People Who Write Science Fiction.* New York: Berkley Books, 1980, 155.
[6] Lawrence Sutin, *Divine Invasions: A Life of Philip K. Dick.* New York: Citadel Press/Carol Publishing Group, 1991, 221.
[7] Dick, *The Divine Invasion.* 1981; rpt. Vintage/Random House, 1991, 173 (§14).

July 1974 letter: "There were literally hundreds of them; they replaced each other at dazzling speed... I spent over eight hours enjoying one of the most beautiful and exciting and moving sights I've ever seen, conscious that it was a miracle ... *I* was not the author of these graphics. The number alone proved that."[8]

Dick also had a number of vivid dream experiences in which he felt that vital information was transferred to him, but with the exception of scattered phrases he was unable to consciously recall any of this information. Another letter describes these tutelary dreams:

> During sleep I was receiving information in the form of print-outs: words and sentences, letters and names and numbers—sometimes whole pages, sometimes in the form of writing paper and holographic writing, sometimes, oddly, in the form of a baby's cereal box on which all sorts of quite meaningful information which was written and typed, and finally galley proofs held up for me to read which I was told in my dream "contained prophecies about the future," and during the last two weeks a huge book, again and again, with page after page of printed lines.[9]

When Dick did remember words and phrases of this writing, they were often completely incomprehensible to him. He wrote a number of them down phonetically, and later discovered that they were in other languages, most importantly *koine* Greek. In a 1981 interview, Dick claimed "it used Greek words, which I had never heard. I had no idea. *Anake* [*sic, Ananke* probably intended]. I had no knowledge of the word *anake*... I was able to write down sixteen, at least sixteen different Greek words, phonetically."[10] When he wrote down these words, he had no idea of what they meant, and he incorporated this glossolalia (or, as he called it, xenoglossy) into his theories about the "other personality" who may have taken over his mind in 2-3-74.

One startling aspect of Dick's religious experience that has received a good deal of attention from Dick's fans and scholars occurred in August, 1974. The experience led to what Dick believed was a divine healing based on information communicated to him via a "pink beam of light" of unknown origin. He recalls the story in a journal entry c.1977:

---

[8] Quoted in Sutin, *Divine Invasions*, 213.
[9] Quoted in Sutin, *Divine Invasions*, 219.
[10] Rickman, *Last Testament*, 55. Rickman defines "*Anake*" as "astral determinism or fate."

> Sitting with my eyes shut I am listening to "Strawberry Fields." I get up. I open my eyes because the lyrics speak of "Going through life with eyes closed." I look toward the window. Light blinds me; my head suddenly aches. My eyes close & I see strange strawberry ice cream pink. At the same instant knowledge is transferred to me. I go into the bedroom where [Phil's wife] Tessa is changing Chrissy [Christopher, Dick's son, who was just over a year old at the time] & I recite what has been conveyed to me: that he has an undetected birth defect & must be taken to the doctor at once & scheduled for surgery.[11]

Dick has elsewhere stated that he not only knew that his son had an undiagnosed birth defect, but that the "pink beam" told him precisely what kind—a right inguinal hernia.[12] In a 1975 letter, Dick claims that the beam's source "absolutely accurately diagnosed Christopher's birth defect."[13] Dick identifies this revelation of unknown information as a miracle, and further, a miracle through which the source of his experiences healed his son. This event is a source of great skepticism among those familiar with Dick's experiences, and it may be less of a miracle then Dick made it seem. Tessa Dick, his wife at the time of the experience and the mother of Christopher, has elsewhere stated that Christopher was an abnormally fussy child, and she had previously suspected that he might have had a hernia.[14] But Dick himself was convinced that the diagnosis was miraculous, and it played a central role in his speculations on the nature and origin of his experience.

These are but a handful of the experiences that Dick reported between 1974 and his death in 1982. An account of all of them would fill thousands of pages—and Dick himself did this. He began taking extensive notes shortly after 2-3-74, researching theological topics in hope of better understanding his experiences. Though they began as notes for a novel, these writings took on an importance of their own to Dick, and eventually grew into the journal he called the *Exegesis*. By his death, the *Exegesis* contained over 8,000 pages of mostly handwritten notes in which he tested theory after theory to explain and explore the countless possible meanings of 2-3-74. Had it been an actual divine revelation, contact with a creature from

---

[11] Quoted in Sutin, *Divine Invasions,* 225.
[12] Rickman, *Last Testament,* 43.
[13] Philip K. Dick. *The Selected Letters of Philip K. Dick, Volume 4: 1975-1976.* Don Herron, ed. Novata, California: Underwood-Miller, 1992, 241.
[14] J. B. Reynolds, "The PKDS Interview With Tessa B. Dick (and Christopher Dick)." *Philip K. Dick Society Newsletter (PKDS)* 13 (February 1987), 4.

another time or planet, or merely the result of psychosis? Dick explored these and countless more theories in the *Exegesis*, writing as much as 150 pages in a single late-night session. But he never came to any definite conclusion about the origin of 2-3-74.

THE *EXEGESIS*

The name Dick gave to his journal of speculations gives us some hints as to how he viewed both his religious experience and his own writing process. That he considered his nightly speculations an exegetical process implies that he believed he was *interpreting a form of scripture*. The *Exegesis* is rife with interpretations of Dick's own novels and stories, which he believed contained hints as to the source of his religious experience and the true nature of reality. A 1978 entry explains: "Buried in my 27 years of writing lies information: in these writings I have told what I knew without knowing what I knew. I know now. . . When I did not know that I knew (or who & what I am) I could speak."[15] In the *Exegesis*, Dick puzzled through meaning after possible meaning of his own work, finding new lenses through which to scrutinize his own oeuvre and new nuances which in his writing which might shed some light on the meaning of 2-3-74. Further, the *Exegesis* quickly became an exegesis of itself, as Dick examined old ideas in the development of new ones. The text did not merely explain; it provided material in need of explanation, which it then recursively, cumulatively interpreted in new and dynamic ways.

In addition to exploring his fiction writing, Dick viewed his experience itself as something to be interpreted in an exegetical manner. He considered it a subject of study and exposition rather than a basis for a definitive framework for interpreting the world. The *Exegesis* was, by its nature, a theoretical work. Dick's main goal in writing it was to test as many theories as possible as to the meaning of his experience, from the mundane to the orthodox to the bizarre and science-fictional. Descriptions of his experiences are inseparably mingled with theorization, and every entry is rich with both firsthand accounts of 2-3-74 and hypotheses about its nature. Paul Williams, Dick's literary executor and friend, says of the *Exegesis* "seen from the

---

[15] Philip K. Dick, *In Pursuit of Valis: Selections From the Exegesis*, Lawrence Sutin, ed. Novato, California: Underwood-Miller, 1991, 157.

perspective of any given page or section it seems borderless, eternal, immeasurable, an endlessly recurring aha! followed by new analyses, new doubts, new questions and possibilities."[16] By contrast, Jay Kinney, one of the first individuals to read the *Exegesis* in anything close to its entirety, says that parts of the *Exegesis* are "boring and even painful exercises, akin to watching a good friend repeatedly bang his head against the wall."[17] Dick never settled on one theory, though his explorations of each are phrased as if he had finally, after years of guesswork, found the truth. He constantly second-guessed himself, expressing theories and counter-theories, often on the same page, and exploring both the validity and doubtfulness of each. One example of this process comes in a 1981 interview with Greg Rickman—Dick first states, in reference to the origin of his experiences, "I just don't think it is the Holy Spirit. I think it's Elijah."[18] But mere minutes later, he claims "It's probably the Holy Spirit," then qualifies the statement, saying, "I don't have any fixed ideas. I just know that some kind of spirit took me over."[19]

Given its theoretical nature, the *Exegesis* was an endless project, notes for a "nonexistent novel that will never get written."[20] Dick would never have run out of theories to explain 2-3-74, or refutations of earlier theories. There was always a new angle from which to view his experience. Lawrence Sutin, in the preface to the only published volume of *Exegesis* excerpts to date, states that "Dick's analyses frequently cast light on the dilemmas of absolute knowledge and absolute being: the light cast is the presentation of multifold possibilities where once stood only 'official' reality. . . Dick never pretended that he had found The Truth (or not for very long, at any rate)."[21] Any attempt at summarizing the *Exegesis* must keep in mind that, with very few exceptions, every statement and theory in the journal is very likely questioned, if not completely contradicted, elsewhere in Dick's notes.

---

[16] Paul Williams, "Editor's note to 'An Excerpt From the Exegesis,'" *PKDS* 12 (October 1986), p. 5.
[17] Jay Kinney, "Summary of the Exegesis Based on Preliminary Forays," *PKDS* 3 (1984), p. 13.
[18] Rickman, *Last Testament*, 60.
[19] Rickman, *Last Testament*, 61.
[20] Rickman, *Last Testament*, 1.
[21] Lawrence Sutin, "On the Exegesis of Philip K. Dick." Dick, *In Pursuit of Valis*, xi.

This is not to say that Dick didn't think there *was* a truth behind 2-3-74. Rather, he felt that the truth was somehow embedded in the actual process of developing new theories, as will be discussed in more detail below. In a way, Dick believed in all of his theories, embodying William Blake's statement that "Every thing possible to be believ'd is an image of truth."[22] The fact that Dick never held to any one conclusion for longer than a few months—or, in many cases, minutes—does not mean that he did not believe them. He saw a fundamental vitality in every theory he tested, as Paul Williams explains: "He was a passionate seeker of truth; and he found it, explored it, and expressed it, not at the end of the path, but at every possible station along the way."[23] Dick's religious writing is ultimately heterodox and syncretistic, because he accepted, at least temporarily, every theory that offered him some form of insight into his experiences.

But in analyzing Dick's religious thought, how can we tell how seriously he took a given theory? If he believed every theory he put forth while he formulated it, how can we select what portions of the consistently self-contradictory *Exegesis* to actual consider as Dick's "actual beliefs?" It is ultimately necessary to consider the frequency with which Dick discussed a given concept or system: did he merely toy with the idea once and quickly reject it? Did he incorporate it into his speculations for a few months, and then slowly phase it out in favor of a new framework? Or did use it as a basis for his speculations throughout the entire eight years of his *Exegesis*? These questions are difficult to answer given the small number of published *Exegesis* excerpts, but nonetheless several trends are apparent in both these excerpts and reports from those who have read extensively in the unpublished portions of the *Exegesis*. Dick's theoretical explorations must be viewed in the context of the *Exegesis* as a whole. No statement can be simply taken at face value; rather it must be considered in reference to the countless other statements Dick made—and usually rejected—in his eight years of nightly journal-keeping.

---

[22] William Blake, *Complete Poetry and Prose of William Blake, Newly Revised Edition*, ed. David V. Erdman. New York: Anchor Books/Doubleday, 1988, 37. In a 1979 letter, Dick stated that he had "stayed away from Blake because I know, from what a number of people have told me, that I am working out in my writing a number of themes which he developed, so I want to avoid cribbing from him" (*Selected Letters, vol. 5: 1977-1979*, 239).

[23] Paul Williams, *Only Apparently Real: The World of Philip K. Dick*. New York: Arbor House, 1986, 166.

Certain trends emerge when the *Exegesis* is considered as a divided whole, rather than a haphazard and disconnected series of notes. A number of themes arise to which Dick returned frequently, and these can sometimes be considered the standards by which he measured other theories. Some of these themes become clear in the *Exegesis*' descriptive passages, such as this March 1975 entry in which Dick both describes the development of his experience and considers its redemptive meaning:

> March 16, 1974: It appeared—in vivid fire, with shining colors and balanced patterns—and released me from every thrall, inner and outer.
>
> March 18, 1974: It, from inside me, looked out and saw the world did not compute, that I—and it—had been lied to. It denied the reality, and power, and authenticity of the world, saying, "This cannot exist; it cannot exist."
>
> March 20, 1974: It seized me entirely, lifting me from the limitations of the space-time matrix; it mastered me as, at the same instant, I knew that the world around me was cardboard, a fake. Through its power I saw suddenly the universe as it was; through its power of perception I saw what really existed, and through its power of no-thought decision, I acted to *free myself*. It took on in battle, as a champion of all human spirits in thrall, every evil, every Iron Imprisoning thing.
>
> [...] August 1974: ...When it left me, it left me as a free person, a physically and mentally healed person who had seen reality suddenly, in a flash, at the moment of greatest peril and pain and despair; it had loaned me its power and it had set right what had by degrees become wrong over God knows how long.[24]

As this entry shows, Dick extrapolated from his experience that "reality," as we perceive it, is not *real*—there is an absolute truth which we are normally unable to perceive. Dick's cosmology thus appears to be primarily dualistic in the Platonic sense: it relies on a division between an illusory reality in which we experience our day-to-day existence and the eternal, actual existence—the truly real—that underlies it. Further, the world we can perceive is supposed to be in line with this absolute reality, but something has gone wrong to cause it to deviate from its intended form. Dick views the phenomenal world as something from which we need to be saved; the veil of illusion is ultimately detrimental to us. This is one of several themes that

---

[24] Quoted in Sutin, "On the Exegesis of Philip K. Dick." Dick, *In Pursuit of Valis*, ix.

run throughout the entire *Exegesis*. In all of his speculations, Dick worked from the basis that there is more to reality than what we perceive. From this framework, Dick worked out hypotheses as to what it is, exactly, that enacts this salvation—is it the Holy Spirit? The prophet Elijah? Zeus or Dionysus? A benevolent species of extraterrestrials? Jesus Christ? In eight years of writing the *Exegesis* Dick tested theories based on all of these entities and more, and considered them all plausible in turn. In a 1975 interview, Dick stated "I am inevitably persuaded by every argument that is brought to bear,"[25] and the *Exegesis* contains a near-infinite number of thoroughly explored theories.

COMMUNICATING THE EXPERIENCE: THE VALIS TRILOGY

Based on 2-3-74 and the further experience of writing the *Exegesis*, Philip K. Dick wrote his final three novels—*VALIS, The Divine Invasion,* and *The Transmigration of Timothy Archer,* often collectively termed "The *VALIS* Trilogy."[26] The novels are highly theological, exploring some of the themes of the *Exegesis* and placing some of Dick's experiences in a fictional framework. The first volume, *VALIS*, is largely autobiographical; the first half of the novel is a more-or-less direct account 2-3-74 and the events that directly preceded it. The novel tells the story of Horselover Fat (the name is a translation into English of the respective Greek and German roots of "Philip Dick"), and his experience of what is either a mystical experience or a psychotic episode. We hear of Fat's experiences in the third-person narration of a character named "Phil Dick" who is skeptical about the nature of Fat's experiences. Early in the book, the narrator states "I am Horselover Fat, and I am writing this in the third person to gain much-needed objectivity."[27] The combined character has experienced a psychotic break and is split into two characters, the mystic and the skeptic. In addition to this narration, the novel contains extensive philosophical passages, most of them based on excerpts

---

[25] Platt, *Dream Makers*, 150.
[26] There is some debate in both scholarship and fandom over whether or not the three books form a trilogy at all. With the exception of a brief reference to the events of *VALIS* in *The Divine Invasion*, none of the books contains any significantly direct connection to any other. Nonetheless, Dick himself referred to the books as a trilogy by right of their shared philosophical themes.
[27] Philip K. Dick, *VALIS*, 11 (§1).

from Fat's own *Exegesis*, here called "Tractates: Cryptica Scriptura." Some of these entries were edited directly from Dick's *Exegesis*, most were written exclusively for the novel though based on themes from Dick's notes. In addition to these firsthand accounts of Fat's experience, the book contains a constant commentary and dialog from other characters—Phil Dick, the narrator, and Kevin and David, based on Dick's friends and fellow SF writers K. W. Jeter and Tim Powers. The character Phil Dick consistently questions the authenticity of Fat's experiences, referring to Fat as a lunatic and the *Exegesis* as "the furtive act of a deranged person."[28] He describes the events of Fat's life following the suicide of one of his friends: his mystical experience/nervous breakdown, his institutionalization, and his search, sometimes assisted and sometimes held back by his friends, for the Savior whom he believes is soon to be reborn.

Shortly after this novel, Dick wrote *The Divine Invasion*, a stylistic return to his SF of the sixties that also incorporated the religious speculations of *VALIS*, and *The Transmigration of Timothy Archer*, a "mainstream" (that is, non-SF) novel that explores, in a fictionalized manner, the life and death of Dick's friend, the Episcopal Bishop James A. Pike. SF writer and literary critic Kim Stanley Robinson has described the *VALIS* Trilogy in terms of *VALIS*' split between Horselover Fat and Phil Dick. He proposes "that *The Divine Invasion*, the science fiction novel, is the book written by Horselover Fat, while *The Transmigration of Timothy Archer*, the realist novel, is the book written by 'Phil Dick.'"[29] This is a useful distinction, and explains well the many differences between the two novels. *The Divine Invasion* is a somewhat scattered and confusing book, an only partially successful attempt to place the religious themes of *VALIS* and 2-3-74 in a more overtly science fictional setting. *The Transmigration of Timothy Archer*, on the other hand, is a concise and powerful character study of the title character. It also offers a wonderful exploration of its narrator, Angel Archer, who is Timothy's daughter-in-law. In a manner similar to the narrator's scrutiny of Fat in *VALIS*, Angel traces Timothy's psychological development (or decline) following his son's suicide, leading ultimately to his search for the truth about the historical Jesus in a Palestinian desert—a search that ultimately kills him.

---

[28] Dick, *VALIS*, 22 (§2).
[29] Kim Stanley Robinson, *The Novels of Philip K. Dick*. Ann Arbor, Michigan: UMI Research Press, 1984, 111.

Transmigration is also more skeptical regarding theological themes, echoing the often skeptical narration of *VALIS*. In *The Divine Invasion*, we are told early on that Emmanuel, the protagonist's son, is the reborn Savior; for much of the novel, it seems that Emmanuel himself is the only one who does not know. In *Archer*, nothing is so clear-cut—Timothy Archer's theories are never verified, and Angel, like Phil in *VALIS*, constantly questions the value of any theological theory that could lead to suffering or, in Timothy's case, death. There is no real resolution about the theological issues raised in the book, but the reader is left with the distinct feeling that there was something real behind Tim's speculations. The *VALIS* Trilogy ends on an unresolved note—like the *Exegesis*, it makes no final claims, but asks as many questions as it can. The reader is left believing that something has happened, that there is some value in the religious speculations of the characters and their author, but it is impossible to say what exactly that value is.

PHILOSOPHICAL CONCERNS IN DICK'S WRITING BEFORE 2-3-74

2-3-74 sparked Dick's most serious religious thinking, but it was not the first time that religious ideas entered his work. Beginning with his earliest stories and novels, his "science" fiction was based on philosophical themes rather than scientific ones, and in a 1981 *Exegesis* entry he describes his oeuvre: "I am basically analytical, not creative; my writing is simply a creative way of handling analysis. I am a fictionalizing philosopher, not a novelist; my novel & story-writing ability is employed as a means to formulate my perception. The core of my writing is not art but *truth*."[30] Religion plays an important role in all his work: his first published novel, *Solar Lottery*, has a major subplot based on a religious sect that believes that Heaven is a tenth planet in our solar system. Similarly, *The Cosmic Puppets*, written before *Solar Lottery* but published a year later, is the story of a small town torn apart by the battle between Good and Evil, personified in the Zoroastrian deities Ormazd and Ahriman.[31]

Despite the centrality of religious and philosophical themes in much of his work, Dick was often skeptical about attempts to make SF religious.

---

[30] Dick, *In Pursuit of Valis*, 161. Emphasis in original.
[31] Phil's original title for this novel—*A Glass of Darkness*—was a reference to 1 Corinthians; the allusion reappeared over twenty years later in his superb anti-drug novel *A Scanner Darkly*.

In a 1966 essay, he writes: "Religion ought never to show up in SF except from a sociological standpoint . . . God per se, as a character, ruins a good SF story; and this is as true of my own stuff as anyone else's."[32] Dick had lived for a number of years in Berkeley, where atheism was the norm: "I had [a] Berkeley anti-religious attitude, which a lot of people have now. All you have to do is mention God, and they just barf."[33] But this had not always been Dick's attitude, and religion had, in fact, been quite important to him earlier in life. His parents, who were Quakers, were not particularly devout Christians, but nonetheless Dick came to be fascinated with religion at a fairly young age. In a 1982 interview, he describes one part of this fascination:

> When I was in junior high school there was a soap opera on daytime radio called "The Light of the World," a story of the Bible and they dramatized part of the Bible. I happened to start listening during the part about Elijah. And I started reading the Bible and I read that part about Elijah. And it was my greatest wish in the world of anything was to hear that low murmuring voice that Elijah heard. The voice of the Lord.[34]

Dick got his wish within a few years—on a high school physics exam, he was unable to remember the principle for the displacement of water, on which most of the exam was based. As time ran out, he began to pray, the results of which Dick describes in a 1977 letter: "All at once this lovely inner voice had come on, had fully and very calmly explained the scientific formula—I got all eight of the answers right, based on what the voice had told me."[35] Dick heard this voice again during and after 2-3-74, and in the *Exegesis* he referred to it as the "A.I. Voice," because it sounded like an artificial intelligence rather than a human being. He frequently compared the A.I. Voice to the "still small voice" Elijah hears in 1 Kings 19:12.

Though this religious desire was overwhelmed by the atheism of his Berkeley years, Dick eventually joined the Episcopal Church in 1963. In a 1981 interview he claims that the conversion itself was not a major event, but Dick was fascinated with the theological matters it introduced him to: "My conversion. . . was really not such a big deal. It was only after I began

---

[32] Philip K. Dick, "Will the Atomic Bomb Ever be Perfected, and if so, What Becomes of Robert Heinlein?" in *Shifting Realities*, 58.
[33] Rickman, *Last Testament*, 8-9.
[34] Rickman, *Last Testament*, 221.
[35] Dick, *Selected Letters vol. 5: 1977-1979*, 57.

to study the doctrine of transubstantiation in the Eucharist that I began to get into the mystical aspects of it. It was more a metaphysical mystic thing than a doctrine."[36] Nancy Hackett, Dick's fourth wife, met him shortly after he joined the church, and claims that "he took this very seriously, although he mixed many other religions and philosophies with it. He was fond of integrating various kinds of knowledge, and would often come up with his own theories."[37] Tessa Dick, who was married to Phil during the 2-3-74 experiences, further explains that "Phil was often unorthodox, even heretical, but he was never un-Christian... he believed that the only way to salvation is through Christ."[38] Dick's Christianity did not always show through explicitly in his writing, but his fascination with philosophical theories and systems did.

In a 1978 essay, Dick divided his philosophical concerns into two main questions: "The two topics that fascinate me are 'What is reality?' and 'What constitutes the authentic human being?' Over the twenty-seven years in which I have published novels and stories I have investigated those two interrelated topics over and over again... What are we? What is it that surrounds us, that we call the not-me, or the empirical or phenomenal world?"[39] Dick searched for answers to these two questions, testing theory after theory in his writing over his thirty-year writing career. In novels such as *The Penultimate Truth*, in which a small elite holds its power over the majority by forcing them to hide in massive bomb shelters from a war that has been over for years, and *The Simulacra*, in which the country's President is actually an android figurehead whose human wife holds the actual power, Dick explored the questions of the nature of reality and humanity. To one of them—the question of humanity—he soon found an answer.

What is "human"?

One of Dick's goals was to ascertain what it is that, in a world where mechanical constructs increasingly resemble human beings and human beings increasingly act like machines, separates the categories of "human"

---

[36] Rickman, *Last Testament*, 9.
[37] Nancy Hackett, "Letter to The Philip K Dick Society," PKDS 16 (January 1988), p.4.
[38] Tessa B. Dick "Letter to The Philip K. Dick Society," PKDS 17 (April 1988), p.12.
[39] Dick, "How to Build a Universe," in *Shifting Realities*, 260.

on one hand and "non-human" or "android" on the other. In his SF, Dick posits a future in which a robot may be more authentically human than a biological person—humanity, for him, depends not on biology, but on action and emotion. In his earliest stories, his definition was already beginning to take shape: "I was casting about in an effort to contrast the truly human from what I was later to call the 'android or reflex machine' that looks human but is not . . . It has to do with empathy, or, as it was called in earlier times, *caritas* or *agape*."[40] The human mind is that which is able to show kindness to the beings around it. The authentic human will do anything, no matter the risk to itself, to protect the beings around it that cannot protect themselves. Dick's ultimate loyalty was to humanity: "those who are starving, those who are sick, and those who are in need. . . the *nepioi*, the little ones of the world."[41] Essential to understanding Dick's definition of the human is his definition of the *in*human (or android) mind, and his ideas on what we can do to avoid sinking into the heartlessness and selfishness of the "reflex machine." Dick describes a hypothetical situation in which an individual's humanity is subjugated:

> A native of Africa is said to view his surroundings as pulsing with a purpose, a life, that is actually within himself; once these childish projections are withdrawn, he sees that the world is dead and that life resides solely within himself. When he reaches this sophisticated point he is said to be either mature or sane. Or scientific. But one wonders: Has he not also, in this process, reified—that is, made into a thing—other people? Stones and rocks and trees may now be inanimate for him, but what about his friends? Has he now made them into stones, too?[42]

For Dick it is a matter of absolute spiritual necessity to care for our fellow human beings: to view them as objects instead of equal beings is to cease to be human ourselves.

Perhaps the clearest depiction of the android mind in Dick's work is the title character of the 1964 novel *The Three Stigmata of Palmer Eldritch*. A wealthy industrialist, Eldritch leaves the solar system on a journey of exploration and capitalist expansion. Ten years later, he returns with a hallucinogenic super-drug called Chew-Z which, when taken, isolates the

---

[40] Dick, "'Headnote' for 'Beyond Lies the Wub.'" *Shifting Realities*, 106.
[41] Rickman, *Last Testament*, 155.
[42] Dick, "The Android and the Human." In *Shifting Realities*, 183.

user in a nightmarish world under Eldritch's control. Users of the drug become confined to their hallucinations, and Eldritch eventually overtakes their personal worlds, turning them into mere extensions of himself. Eldritch himself, it turns out, is merely a tool of a mysterious alien deity: "With vast trailing arms he extended from the Proxima Centaurus system to Terra itself, and he was not human; this was not a man who had returned. And he had great power. He could overcome death."[43] Dick has referred to the novel as "a study of absolute evil,"[44] and Palmer Eldritch as "God backward,"[45] the antithesis of the good deity in which Dick came to believe. But what qualities make Eldritch so evil?

Eldritch is the ultimate android—he returns from his journey an evil god, attempting to devour the human population of the solar system in an effort to extend his own life. Eldritch-the-man allowed himself to become the tool of an evil, inhuman power, and then, through the drug Chew-Z, forced others to become extensions of himself, starting with his business rival, Leo Bulero. At one point in the novel, Eldritch expresses his desire to become a planet—not the planet itself, but "everyone on the planet."[46] All Eldritch cares about is the extension of his own temporal and spatial existence, and he is willing to devour countless lives to this end. Dick frequently likens the taking of Chew-Z to the miracle of transubstantiation. Just as the members of the Church partake of and become extensions of Christ's immortal body, the Martian colonists in *The Three Stigmata* partake of and become Eldritch's body.[47] In one character's hallucination, Eldritch explains this effect of the drug: "Well, you got what St. Paul promises. . . you're no longer clothed in a perishable fleshly body—you've put on an ethereal body in its place."[48] The difference is that Christ's Eucharist exists for the immortality and salvation of humanity, whereas Eldritch's Eucharist serves only Eldritch himself, allowing *him* immortality at the expense of all other life. He is wholly incapable of empathy—he views others as objects, tools to be incorporated into his own empty being.

---

[43] Philip K. Dick, *The Three Stigmata of Palmer Eldritch*. 1965; rpt. New York: Vintage/Random House, 1991, 203 (§12).
[44] Dick, "The Android and the Human." In *Shifting Realties*, 206.
[45] Dick, *In Pursuit of Valis*, 21.
[46] Dick, *Three Stigmata*, 204 (§12).
[47] Dick, *Selected Letters 1977-1979*, 134-135.
[48] Dick, *Three Stigmata*, 193 (§11).

DICK AS RELIGIOUS PHILOSOPHER

This failure to treat other beings as equals, as other subjects rather than as objects, is the essence of inhumanity for Dick. The ultimate example of this inhumanity occurred in the Holocaust, a subject on which Dick wrote and spoke extensively. The Holocaust, he says, did not occur because of hatred on the parts of those involved in the killing, but rather because of a bureaucratic system that taught the people in it—even the victims of violence—to treat people as things. In one interview, Dick discusses an account of Jehovah's Witnesses in one concentration camp who, as part of the camp bureaucracy, typed up lists of people who were to be killed each day:

> This is the essence of the unhuman... These Jehovah's Witnesses knew the situation; they knew that they and other people where going to be gassed. And yet they were typing lists, and emptying wastebaskets, whatever, as long as it didn't break some damn ordinance in the Bible like "Thou shalt not salute the flag." They'd go to their deaths rather than salute the flag, and yet they'd type up and carry lists of people who were to be exterminated![49]

The Holocaust, for Dick, is the end result of a way of thinking in which the value of other human beings is disregarded. Biological humans became "reflex machines" when they "became instruments, means rather than ends" of the Nazi party.[50]

Martin Buber, in *I and Thou*, describes a very similar view of human relation, similarly informed by the moral problem of the Holocaust.[51] For Buber there are two worlds in which human beings can exist: the It-world and the You-world. The It-world encompasses the experience of things, the experience that sees all other beings as objects to be used to attain goals. The It-world is "somewhat reliable; it has density and duration... it is your object and remains that, according to your pleasure—and remains primally alien both outside and inside you."[52] The You-world, on the other hand, is the world of pure relation: of recognizing another being *as a being*, and

---

[49] Apel, *The Dream Connection*, 36-37.
[50] Dick, "The Android and the Human." In *Shifting Realities*, 187.
[51] Dick was familiar with Buber, though he rarely cites him directly. Interestingly, he attributes the above story of Jehovah's Witnesses in concentration camps to the memoirs of Paula Buber, Martin Buber's wife (Apel, *The Dream Connection*, 36).
[52] Martin Buber, *I and Thou*. Trans. Walter Kaufman. New York: Simon and Schuster, 1970, 82-83.

sharing "a pure natural association, a flowing toward each other."[53] This is the ultimate expression of humanity: the realization that everything one experiences can be encountered as a You rather than an It, and through this relation entering into a relation with "the eternal You." The relation is, on many levels, an empathic understanding: seeing the subjectivity of another being, rather than viewing it as a mere object. And though Buber believes it is necessary for our survival that we live in the It-world to a certain degree, it is the I-You encounter that makes us human: "without It a human being cannot live. But whoever lives only with that is not human."[54]

What does it mean for us to live only the world of things? Both Dick and Buber suggest that the pure relation, the understanding of the entire world as alive, is the original state of humankind, and that it is only after society has transformed and isolated us that we are able to view things and people as mere objects. After this transformation, we begin viewing others as things to be used to achieve various ends, and we become things ourselves. Buber writes of such an isolated person: "To be sure, he views the beings around him as so many machines capable of different achievements that have to be calculated and used for the cause. But that is also how he views himself... He treats himself, too, as an It."[55] If we forget the humanity of those around us, then we are bound to forget our own, to view our own selves as a mere means by which to achieve goals. This is precisely what makes Palmer Eldritch "absolute evil"—he views the entire human race as a tool by which to achieve eternal life, but because he has allowed himself to become a tool himself, that life can have no real meaning, no matter how many individuals he comes to inhabit. By losing empathy, we lose our own humanity.

Related to the question of empathy is one of the major themes in Dick's fictional and analytic writing: the question of the division between sanity and insanity. The inability to view one's fellow human beings as other individuals, even if it is often conventionally accepted, is characteristic of insanity. In one interview, Dick explained:

> What's lacking is a *sense of perspective*, a sense of proportion. If you pick up your instructions that morning when you go to work and it says, "Twenty people will be gassed today," and this is typed out and it's all spelled right, and it's on the right form, and this seems fine to you, then what we have here is not just an insidious

---

[53] Buber, *I and Thou*, 76.
[54] Buber, *I and Thou*, 85.
[55] Buber, *I and Thou*, 118.

pathology, but almost, in a way, the heart of true pathology. What we have here is a lack of an emotional grasping of a situation. We have here a purely mechanical mind, a metal sphere rotating without any contact with the earth or other humans.[56]

Sanity, for Dick, means grasping the emotional gravity of a situation, and reacting to it morally—if asked to do something that is *wrong*, that requires harming the innocent or oneself, then the sane mind will stop. It will not allow itself to cause unnecessary injury to its fellow humans, for it understands that they, too, *are* humans. If asked to cause an unjust act, the sane human being will balk, refusing to commit the moral atrocity of harming its fellow beings. Thus Dick views the bureaucratic, android mind as insane—it does *not* grasp the moral gravity of dire situations, because for it, all things are simply things. The "scientific man" sees no moral difference between a human and a stone; both, to him, are simply objects to be either used or ignored. The android mind is isolated; it is unable to perceive any connection between itself and other beings like it. In this it thinks itself superior—it has, as Dick stated in a passage quoted above, "withdrawn its childish projections," and now sees the world as it is, unclouded by emotion. But is this reality? Buber explains: "Where there is no participation, there is no actuality. . . The more directly the You is touched, the more perfect the participation."[57] The deepest level of reality is not things-as-things; it is the eternal You—and this can only be reached through the empathic relation. *Caritas, agape*, empathy, the relation with the eternal You—these are at the core of reality. And it is precisely these that the android mind cannot perceive; hence it is out of touch with reality, and its view of the world is deranged.

Palmer Eldritch is the ultimate deranged mind. Not only does he seem unable to enter into a relation with his fellow human beings, but he isolates them as well, locking them into the same sort of alienation in which he is trapped. He is both deranged and deranging; his method of expansion requires that he turn his victims into beings as inhuman as himself. Buber describes a situation quite applicable to Eldritch: "What has become an It is then taken as an It, experienced and used as an It, employed along with other things for the project of finding one's way in the world, and eventually for the project of 'conquering' the world."[58] But once one begins striving after

---

[56] Apel, *The Dream Connection*, 38.
[57] Buber, *I and Thou*, 113.
[58] Buber, *I and Thou*, 91.

this goal, there is no reason to do it—the being that does the conquering no longer has a self of any real value. It is simply a "rotating metal sphere," an android mind that does not love its fellow beings. And thus Dick, in his speech "The Android and the Human," advises us to retain our humanity as we explore the universe around us: "It is not merely *where* we go, to Alpha Centauri or Betelgeuse, but what we are as we make our pilgrimages there. Our natures will be going there, too. *Ad astra*—but *per hominum*."[59] To the stars—but as men.

What is "reality"?

Dick found an answer to the question of humanity in a world of androids soon after first asking it. The second question—"What is reality?"—Dick dealt with more frequently, in large part because he was not able to reach a definite answer. The roots of this questioning were already apparent in "Roog," the first story Dick sold. It is the story of a dog who, in an effort to protect its human owners, barks at the garbagemen—or, as the dog sees them, "Roogs," alien beings who come "to steal the precious food that the family stores up every day until the heavily constructed metal urn is full. . . [They] steal the harvest just when it's ripe and perfect."[60] In the dog's reality, the garbagemen are cruel aliens—quite different from how the humans view them. But at the end of the story, we learn that the dog may be right as we overhear a bit of the Roogs' conversation, in which they refer to the dog as a "Guardian" and the garbage as "the offering."[61] The story leaves us questioning whose reality is authentic.

This theme recurs in countless Philip K. Dick stories and novels. In the 1957 novel *Eye in the Sky*, the characters, who are unconscious on the floor of a scientific laboratory following a strange accident, take turns inhabiting one another's private worlds, living in the nightmare that is another person's perception of reality. *Ubik*, published in 1969 and often identified as one of Dick's best novels, has a similar basis: the characters are present at an explosion that they believe kills their employer, Greg Runciter, and leaves them unharmed. But in fact, Runciter is the only one to survive the explosion

---

[59] Dick, "The Android and the Human." In *Shifting Realities*, 189.

[60] Dick, "Memories Found in a Bill From a Small Animal Vet." In *Shifting realities*, 25.

[61] Philip K. Dick, "Roog," *The Collected Stories of Philip K. Dick, Vol. 1*. New York: Citadel Twilight/Carol Publishing Group, 1987, 17.

and the other characters are in cryogenic suspension. Their world is beset with entropy. Coffee and cigarettes are stale, buildings are deteriorating, and objects are moving back in time to simpler forms: jet planes become biplanes, televisions turn to radios. Runciter, hoping to save the characters from their collapsing world, attempts to communicate with the dead characters, but because of the strength of their delusion that they are still alive, he cannot do so directly. Instead, he must hide messages in their world in the form of notes in matchboxes, television commercial jingles and, in one of the book's most powerful images, his own face on the currency the characters use. The characters must use a substance called "Ubik," which appears most frequently in the form of an aerosol spraycan, to keep the power of entropy from destroying them as well as the half-life environment around them. In *The Three Stigmata of Palmer Eldritch*, hallucination and reality are inextricably mingled; once Bulero takes Chew-Z, it is impossible to tell if what he and the other characters experience is actually happening or if it is merely a part of the deranged world in which Eldritch has trapped him.

In Dick's reality-questioning stories, he creates a division between two types of universe, which he describes in a 1970 letter to the Australian journal *SF Commentary*: "For each person there are two worlds, the *idios kosmos*, which is a *unique* private world, and the *koinos kosmos*, which literally means *shared* world (just as *idios* means private). No person can tell which parts of his total worldview is *idios kosmos* and which is *koinos kosmos*, except by the achievement of a strong empathetic rapport with other people... The *koinos kosmos* has, in a certain sense, the support of three billion human beings; an *idios kosmos* the support of only one."[62] Dick's work deals with the breakdown of *idios* and *koinos kosmos*, playing on the ultimate ambiguity between the two. In "Roog," is the dog's view of the garbagemen a misunderstanding caused by a language barrier, or a perception of a hidden reality? In *The Three Stigmata of Palmer Eldritch*, which reality is authentic—that of the human characters such as Leo Bulero, or the deadly hallucinations of Eldritch? In Dick's worlds, the "authentic" reality often has little effect on the characters; the *idios kosmos*, be it their

---

[62] Dick, "Letter of Comment." In Bruce Gillespie, ed., *Philip K. Dick: Electric Shepherd*. Melbourne, Australia: Norstrilia, 1975, 31-32.

own or that of another powerful individual, is closer to them, and frequently has a greater ability to cause them harm despite its "hallucinatory" nature.

Dick believed in multiple realities, *idioi kosmoi* without number. But in both his fiction and nonfiction, he frequently posits an absolute reality, an authentic *koinos kosmos* to which the characters seek to return. This is the reason Bulero wants to escape Eldritch's world—though it is powerfully real for him while he is in it, he knows that a world exists that Eldritch has not yet invaded. Dick was profoundly influenced by both Plato and Plotinus, and in a 1980 interview explores this influence: "I came to understand that the human mind could conceive of a realm of which the empirical world was epiphenomenal. Finally I came to believe that in a certain sense the empirical world was not truly real, at least not as real as the archetypal realm beyond it. At this point I despaired of the veracity of sense data."[63] Dick, like Plato, came to consider the world we experience as "semi-real," a limited perception of absolute reality filtered through the thought-system of the individual. In our perception of reality, the truth is inexplicably mixed in with our own psychological projections and presuppositions. But the world as we see it nonetheless contains a portion of the truth: "it has some existence to it, it's not merely a hallucination," it is still a reflection of the ideal Forms even if it is not the Forms themselves.[64] The world we see, according to Dick, is not the real world, but neither is it wholly unreal. He devoted much of his writing to determining where, exactly, these lines are drawn. In this, Dick was more than a novelist—even before 2-3-74, he was actively engaged with philosophical and religious ideas, and his later religious experience merely brought these tendencies to the fore.

---

[63] Frank C. Bertrand, "Philip K. Dick on Philosophy: A Brief Interview." *Niekas* 36, 1988, 22-24. Originally published as "Philip K. Dick et la Philosophie: Une Courte Interview," trans. by Sylvie Laine. *Yellow Submarine* 41, September 1986, 30-31. Reprinted in Philip K. Dick, *The Shifting Realities of Philip K. Dick: Selected Literary and Philosophical Writings*, ed. Lawrence Sutin. New York: Vintage/Random House, 1995, 44-47.

[64] Gregg Rickman, *Philip K. Dick: In His Own Words*. Long Beach, CA: Fragments West/Valentine Press, 1984, 133.

CHAPTER TWO

"A Scanner Darkly": Dick as a Christian Theologian

> *I could have shot for Messiah. You'd better at least be glad I only shot for John the Baptist.*
>
> —Philip K. Dick in interview, 1982[1]

> *For now we see in a mirror, dimly, but then we will see face to face. Now I know only in part; then I will know fully, even as I have been fully known. And now faith, hope, and love abide; these three; and the greatest of these is love.*
>
> —1 Corinthians 13:12-13

VIEWS OF DICK'S RELIGIOUS EXPERIENCE IN PAST SCHOLARSHIP

Dick's SF has received a good deal of critical and scholarly attention. Numerous books and collections of essays are devoted to his writing, as well as two special issues of the critical journal *Science Fiction Studies* (*SFS*) and several fan newsletters. To date, most of the attention Dick has received has been from the standpoint of either SF fandom or of literary and political criticism. The former frequently merely lauds Dick's work as genius, while the latter portrays his novels as either conscious expressions of the postmodern condition or as thinly-veiled Marxist expositions. Dick himself had little to say regarding his fans' opinions of his work—in fact, he often claimed to have had very little contact with his fans, and even seemed surprised to learn that he had any. As for scholarly interpretations of his work, he was frequently very critical of the philosophies that scholars applied to his work, often to the point of outright hostility. He sometimes considered scholarly work on his writing to be a sort of attack, or an attempt

---

[1] Rickman, *Last Testament*, 216.

at subversion, as he explains in a 1978 *Exegesis* entry: "If they couldn't get us to write serious things, they solved the problem by decreeing that what we were writing *was* serious. Taking a pop form as 'serious' is what you do if it won't go away... they get you to submit your S-F writing to them to criticize."[2] Dick did not disapprove of *all* scholarship of his work; in fact, he was quite helpful to some scholars who studied his novels and stories. But if he disagreed with a writer's conclusions about his work and the views expressed in it, his disapproval was extreme.

One example of scholarship of which Dick disapproved is Peter Fitting's article "*Ubik*: The Deconstruction of Bourgeois SF," presented in an issue of *Science Fiction Studies* devoted to Dick in March, 1975.[3] Fitting makes a case for *Ubik* as both a postmodern treatise and the antithesis of the pro-capitalist "representational novel," drawing largely on the book's extensive exploration of the division between subjective and objective reality.[4] In *Ubik*, "reality" is not static; the objects in the book's universe are moving backwards in time and deteriorating. The characters' sense of certainty is eliminated as the world literally falls apart around them. Fitting reads the novel as an allegory of social class, claiming that it "lays bare the principal ways in which SF is used for ideological ends."[5] Further, Fitting interprets the metaphysical aspects of *Ubik* as similarly subversive, describing the novel as "a deconstruction of the *metaphysical ideologies* and the *metaphysical formal implications of the classical bourgeois novel*."[6] Regarding the anti-entropic substance and theological concept of "Ubik," Fitting claims that "although the reality problem is thus posed in metaphysical terms, such expectations by the reader are ultimately frustrated, and metaphysics is rejected."[7] Fitting's final estimation of the novel is that it is a "breakthrough, not only in the sense of the deconstruction of the SF novel, but also of a

---

[2] Dick, *In Pursuit of Valis*, 152.
[3] The article was reprinted in *On Philip K. Dick: 40 Articles From* Science Fiction Studies, from which the paginations in this book are taken.
[4] For a brief summary of *Ubik*, see ch. 2 above.
[5] Peter Fitting, "*Ubik*: The Deconstruction of Bourgeois SF." *Science Fiction Studies* 5, March 1975. Reprinted in R.D. Mullen et. al., eds. *On Philip K. Dick: 40 Articles From Science-Fiction Studies.* Terre Haute and Greencastle, Indiana: SF-TH, Inc., 1992, 41.
[6] Fitting, "*Ubik*," 45, emphasis in original.
[7] Fitting, "*Ubik*," 43.

breaking through the psychological and perceptual confines imposed on us by capitalism."[8] Fitting interprets the unreliable nature of reality in *Ubik* as the denial of any ontology that posits a reality beyond individual perception, and also as a critique of temporal, political power structures that attempt to assert control over our perceptions.

But Dick did not restrict his views of his own work to interpretations such as this, and analyses that neglect to look beyond a socio-political meaning are limited at best. Dick's critiques of such analyses were often quite harsh; in a 1974 letter, Dick states that "I've been going through the three ["Marxist" papers on his works, among them Fitting's] that I have and they're so shoddy and near-worthless that for a time I gave up and felt it wasn't worth it."[9] Alexander Star, in his overview of Dick's work, expresses the less-passionate opinion that "Marxist and postmodern readings of Dick's work are often informative; his novels do have more than their share of simulacra and spectacles, fractured identities and postindustrial proletariats. But these readings do not do justice either to his insistence on compassion as a stabilizing force or to his earnest search for an 'absolute reality.'"[10] Even in the novels in which he questions reality with great intensity, Dick *does* posit an absolute reality abiding beneath the unreal phenomenal world: in *Ubik*, despite Fitting's claims to the contrary, the substance Ubik is posited as a link to an absolute reality, if not that absolute reality itself. The claim of Ubik as an absolute item is evidenced both by its power in the narrative itself and by the epigraph to the final chapter, in which Ubik itself speaks in the terms of Judeo-Christian theology: "I am Ubik. Before the universe was, I am. I made the suns. I made the worlds. . . I am the word and my name is never spoken, the name which no one knows."[11] In nearly all of Dick's own analyses of *Ubik*, he begins with a religious interpretation, likening his concept of Ubik to Christian concepts such as *logos* and the Holy Spirit.

---

[8] Fitting, "*Ubik*," 46.
[9] Philip K. Dick, *The Selected Letters of Philip K. Dick: 1974*, ed. Paul Williams. Novata, California: Underwood-Miller, 1991. 148. Despite his deep interest in Greek and Christian philosophy, Dick was no expert on 20th-Century thought, and thus here and elsewhere he calls deconstructionist critiques "Marxist." I have kept the term here in keeping with his own estimation of such works—by 1974, Dick was staunchly anti-Communist, and so his references to such works as "Marxist" shows the degree of his distaste—and also because Fitting's article itself *does* include a Marxist slant in addition to its deconstructionist base.
[10] Alexander Star, "The God in the Trash." *New Republic* December 6, 1993, 39.
[11] Philip K. Dick, *Ubik*. 1969; rpt. New York: Vintage/Random House, 1991, 215 (§17).

Despite Fitting's insistence that metaphysics are rejected in *Ubik*, Dick himself never rejected religious interpretations of his writing, and seems to have thought such interpretations more valuable than more secular, political analyses.

Dick occasionally expressed his own rejection of political interpretations of his work in harsh terms. In a 1974 letter, Dick writes: "I am quite theologically inclined, as *all* critics of my works who are not extreme left-wing irrationally inclined recognize, and theological matter, under science fiction neologisms[,] appear[s] in most if not all of my writing."[12] But most of the scholarly criticism of Dick's writing thus far has played down the importance of philosophy and religion in his fiction. One of Dick's earliest works to emphasize philosophical subjects is the 1962 novel *The Man in the High Castle*. The novel is deeply rooted of religion and philosophy, specifically dealing with the Chinese divination text the *I Ching* and the related Taoist concepts of *yin* and *yang*. *The Man in the High Castle* occurs in an alternate present in which Germany and Japan won the Second World War, in a North America divided between the two nations. Much of the action occurs on the Japanese-dominated West Coast, where the *I Ching* is central to all of the characters' lives. The very plot of the novel was determined by *I Ching* readings, as Dick explains in a 1976 radio interview: "Every time my people would cast a hexagram, I actually cast it for them and let them proceed on the basis of the advice given."[13] The Taoist influence shows through in the novel's discussions of the interplay of yin and yang; one character describes the Nazi-dominated Earth of the novel as the "yin world, in its most melancholy aspect."[14] The world of the novel is unbalanced, and they way in which it can be redeemed is not through political disruption of the German and Japanese governments, but rather through a religious or spiritual transformation. One character experiences such a transformation late in the novel, and is brought into the real world, that of the reader. But most of the critical analyses of this book have made only a brief reference to the centrality of Chinese philosophical concepts in

---

[12] Dick, *Selected Letters: 1974*, 40.

[13] Philip K. Dick, "The Mainstream that Through the Ghetto Flows: An Interview With Philip K. Dick." *Missouri Review* 7 no. 2 (Winter 1984), p. 172.

[14] Philip K. Dick, *The Man in the High Castle*. New York: G.P. Putnam's Sons, 1962, 214 (§14).

the novel, instead choosing to focus on the novel's depiction of the German and Japanese governments. Patricia Warrick, in an essay devoted to the Taoist aspects of the novel, explains: "[*The Man in the High Castle*] is often read as a political novel exploring fascism. Strangely enough, the central role of Oriental philosophy in the novel is ignored by critics. . . [But] the central tension of the novel, essential to the narrative suspense, is the encounter of fascism and Taoism."[15] Warrick's article is the exception, however, not the rule: most of the critical attention Dick's work has received has focused on political ideology and the methods of modern literary criticism, and thus the religious aspects of his work have often been played down or ignored entirely.

DICK'S HERESIES: MODERN GNOSTIC, OR FUTURISTIC CHRISTIAN?

One symptom of this selective scholarship is that Dick's most overtly religious writing, most importantly the *Exegesis* and other religious non-fiction, has not received more than passing attention in the field of religious studies. Because of this, Dick's religious thought is often grossly oversimplified. Many of the literary scholars who have studied Dick's work describe his religious writing as "Gnostic," using that designation as a starting point and rarely questioning the term and whether it is applicable in Dick's case. Those who apply this term to the *Exegesis* and the *VALIS* Trilogy are likely not aware of the controversy among religion scholars regarding the term "gnosticism." This term is used to describe a large number of religious movements, particularly in early Christianity, the specific beliefs of which vary greatly. Hans Jonas has given a definition of the category as "a dualistic transcendent religion of salvation," and explores a number of communities in the first few centuries of Christianity, not necessarily linked to one another in any direct manner, that fit this description well.[16] Though many scholars feel that the term "gnosticism"

---

[15] Patricia Warrick, "The Encounter of Taoism and Fascism in *The Man in the High Castle*." *Science Fiction Studies* 21, July 1980. Reprinted in R.D. Mullen et. al., eds. *On Philip K. Dick: 40 Articles From Science-Fiction Studies*. Terre Haute and Greencastle, Indiana: SF-TH, Inc., 1992, 74.

[16] Hans Jonas, *The Gnostic Religion: The Message of the Alien God and the Beginnings of Christianity, Second Edition, revised*. Boston: Beacon Press, 1963, 32, emphasis removed.

can be used as a useful category for describing a number of belief-systems in the first few centuries of Christianity, others feel that the term generalizes a number of heterogeneous religious communities and obscures the broad differences between them. Michael Allen Williams, one critic of the term, claims that it "has become such a protean label that it has all but lost any reliably identifiable meaning for the larger reading public."[17] Though many consider this term a useful descriptor of diverse traditions, it is unquestionably controversial in the field of religious studies. Given the problematic nature of the category, referring to Dick's religious thought as gnostic does not explain or summarize his concepts, but rather places them into an unclear framework, and attempts to gnosticize his work may even contribute to the lack of clarity in that category's boundaries.

Much of the scholarship regarding Dick's religious experience and the fiction based on it fails to recognize this controversy, as well as the complexity of Dick's theological thought. Some scholars have treated his "gnosticism" as adherence, or near-adherence, to a specific ancient religion. Robert Galbreath, in his survey of the religious themes in *VALIS*, identifies views held by some, but not all, of the sects grouped under the gnostic banner as key tenets of the "philosophical core... of [the] Gnostic experience."[18] Similarly, Patricia Warrick seems to define Gnostics as any individuals who experience "theophanies in which secret knowledge about the nature of God [is] revealed."[19] This statement is misleading from a categorical standpoint, as it potentially places Christian mystics, Sufis, and Hindu sages in the gnostic category. Jean-Noël Dumont, in his brief exploration of the *VALIS* trilogy, takes a different approach, applying the terms "Gnosis" and "Gnosticism" not just to the trilogy, but to Dick's "entire opus," without qualification or explanation.[20] Since these and other scholars approach the

---

[17] Michael Allen Williams, *Rethinking "Gnosticism": An Argument for Dismantling a Dubious Category*. Princeton: Princeton University Press, 3.

[18] Robert Galbreath, "Salvation-Knowledge: Ironic Gnosticism in *Valis* and *The Flight to Lucifer*." In Gary Wolfe, ed., *Science Fiction Dialogues*. Chicago: Academy Chicago, 1982,117.

[19] Patricia Warrick, "Philip K. Dick's Answers to the Eternal Riddles." In Robert Reilly, ed., *The Transcendent Adventure: Studies of Religion in Science Fiction/ Fantasy*. Westport, Connecticut: Greenwood Press, 1985, 119-120.

[20] Jean-Noël Dumont, "Between Faith and Melancholy: Irony and the Gnostic Meaning of Dick's 'Divine Trilogy.'" *Science Fiction Studies* 45, July 1988. Reprinted in R.D. Mullen et. al., eds. *On Philip K. Dick: 40 Articles From Science-Fiction Studies*. Terre Haute and Greencastle, Indiana: SF-TH, Inc., 1992, 242.

religious themes in Dick's work from the arena of literature rather than religious studies, they seem to be ignorant of the controversy surrounding the terms they use to categorize Dick's religious thought.

Given the theoretical nature of Dick's theological speculations, it is problematic and inaccurate to attempt to find one category that can describe the entire breadth of Dick's metaphysics. Dick *did* frequently call his own ideas as gnostic, and many of his novels contain dualistic cosmologies and theological systems that *do* bear a great resemblance to ideas contained in some of the ancient texts that modern scholarship describes as gnostic. But it is both a mistake and a disservice to the rich variety of Dick's religious ideas to describe his entire experience and process of interpretation so simply, with a single categorical designation. Dick's self-designations as gnostic were nearly always followed by lengthy qualification, and, as with all of his self-designations, they were always temporary, changing as he developed new theories. Further, gnostic ideas were not the only religious concepts Dick explored; in one *Exegesis* entry a gnostic-dualist cosmology is illustrated with a yin-yang, a Taoist symbol.[21] In many other places Dick mixed gnostic interpretations his own work with explicit references to Buddhism, orthodox Christianity, Platonic philosophy and Hindu Vedanta, among many other

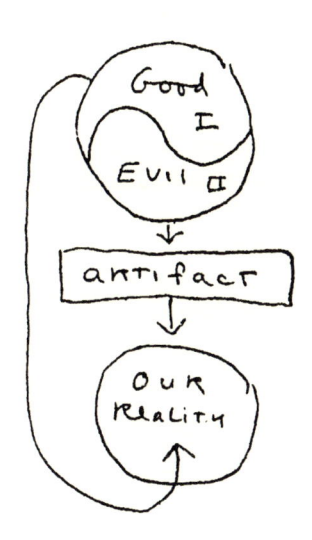

---

[21] Dick, *In Pursuit of Valis*, 72.

philosophical systems. In countless other entries he explores his experience without reference to gnosticism at all. Lorenzo DiTomasso rightly claims that, in Dick's religious novels but also in the *Exegesis*, "there is more here than straightforward dualism... [Rather, it is] Dick's conflation of similar elements of different philosophies."[22] The explorations of Dick's religious ideas published so far tend to take for granted his occasional self-designation as gnostic, an understandable confusion given Dick's apparent (but very temporary) conviction that each theory he tested was the truth. Michel Desjardins, a religion scholar who has explored some of the religious themes in Dick's novels, claims that Dick's reading of the Nag Hammadi texts "made him think that the revelatory light had been *nothing else but ancient gnosticism redivivus.*"[23] This summation fails to acknowledge the centrality of the theoretical process in the *Exegesis*: the speculations that Dick *did* call Gnostic are by no means final, and to take them as such is to forget the theoretical nature of Dick's religious writing.

Fortunately, several scholars have recognized that the diversity of Dick's religious ideas ranges far beyond gnosticism. Lorenzo DiTomasso, who has written several articles on religious themes in Dick's writing, criticizes scholars who attempt to attribute one system of thought to Dick's entire body of religious fiction: "So many Dick scholars take for granted the view that his philosophy is static or entirely coherent. It is not, and sometimes not even within the context of a single novel."[24] Iouan Couliano, in *The Tree of Gnosis*, similarly criticizes the belief that Dick is simply a "modern gnostic," though this criticism from the arena of the study of gnosticism rather than that of SF: "A closer look at the novel [*The Divine Invasion*] shows that, indeed, Dick took inspiration from Jewish and Jewish-Christian apocalyptic literature... yet his novel... makes no use of gnostic material."[25] Similarly,

---

[22] Lorenzo Ditomasso, "Gnosticism and Dualism in the Early Fiction of Philip K. Dick." *Science Fiction Studies* vol. 28 (Spring 2001), 54.

[23] Michel Desjardins, "Retrofitting Gnosticism: Philip K. Dick and Christian Origins." In Tina Pippin and George Aichele, eds., *Violence, Utopia, and the Kingdom of God.* London and New York: Routledge, 1998, 126, emphasis added.

[24] Lorenzo DiTommaso, "Lorenzo DiTomasso on Rossi (Letter to *Extrapolation*)." *Extrapolation* 42 no. 1 (Spring 2001), 96.

[25] Ioan P. Couliano, *The Tree of Gnosis: Gnostic Mythology from Early Christianity to Modern Nihilism*. Trans. H.S. Wiesner and Ioan P. Couliano. San Francisco: HarperSanFrancisco, 1990, 262. *The Divine Invasion* seems to be the only novel of Dick's that Couliano has read; his discussion would likely have been more detailed had he instead read *VALIS*, which directly refers to the Nag Hammadi codices and

Umberto Rossi, who is less familiar with gnostic systems than Couliano but has read more widely in Dick's opus, states that although "there are works of his that have a definitely Gnostic taste... there are other traditions in Dick's fictional world, and [the] Christian mainstream... contributed to the making of him and his opus as well."[26] Much of what has been identified as gnostic in Dick's work is just as easily—and often more convincingly—identifiable as Christian.

And it is to Christianity that most of Dick's qualifications eventually return. A footnote Dick wrote to a 1981 *Exegesis* entry states: "After I wrote this (4 a.m.) I went to bed thinking, 'this is Gnosticism for sure.' The explanation almost fits—*almost*, & yet—it occurred to me then that a much simpler & much more convincing explanation would be that *it was Christ*, the real presence of the actual Christ & an expression of the power of Christ to bind & to loosen, to save, Christ as pantocrator & eschatological judge."[27] After lengthy discussions of the gnostic idea of an evil demiurge as the creator of our universe, Dick here returns to Christian doctrine: Christ as the world's sole creator, redeemer and judge. Countless similar comments can be found elsewhere in the *Exegesis*, such as the statement, written in 1981 regarding the source of 2-3-74, that "there can be no doubt that it is the Christian God whom Christ called '*Abba*.'"[28] A 1975 entry directly contradicts a dualistic interpretation of Dick's experience in favor of a distinctly Christian monotheism: "This is not an evil world, as Mani supposed. There is a good world under the evil. The evil is somehow superimposed over it (Maya), and when stripped away, pristine glowing creation is visible... [The] veils of evil must be stripped or washed away (waking up, the washing away by the blood of the Lamb, baptism, etc). To awaken is to awaken to truth, also to beauty: to unity."[29] This passages explicitly rejects Manicheism, a religion that drew on may Gnostic concepts, as the references to the Eucharist and baptism suggest. Despite his occasional self-designations as Gnostic, Dick's

---

gnosticism, and even quotes a Nag Hammadi text. Nonetheless, his statement stands true: Dick's sources range far beyond gnostic texts, and the overall trend of his religious thought is pluralistic.

[26] Umberto Rossi, "Umberto Rossi on DiTomasso (Letter to *Extrapolation*)." *Extrapolation* 42 no. 1 (Spring 2001), 91.

[27] Dick, *In Pursuit of Valis*, 247.

[28] Dick, *In Pursuit of Valis*, 115.

[29] Dick, *In Pursuit of Valis*, 250.

religious writing is rife with powerful, and powerfully supported, Christian interpretations of his experience.

But are these exegeses merely additional theories to be played with, believed for a time, and eventually rejected? There is ample evidence to suggest that the Christian themes in Dick's writings on religious topics are more deeply-rooted than the countless other theories Dick considered. Biographical evidence from those who knew Dick depict a devout, if open-minded, Episcopalian, a firm believer in Christian theology and the authority of the canonical Christian scriptures. Dick's fifth and final wife, Tessa, claims that "I remember quite clearly that Phil always expressed a belief in Christ... I am tired of people proclaiming that, ... because his religious beliefs were strange, he could not possibly have been a Christian."[30] Dick's conversion to Episcopalianism in 1963 seems to have been sincere, even if he was often critical about the actual politics of that, or any other, religious institution. But despite these criticisms, Dick remained a member of the Church, and as his family and friends attest, he truly believed in the salvific power of Christ.

Many of his ideas were, of course, heretical, but even in his most dualistic explorations he never questioned the power and authority of Christ. *VALIS*—which is more commonly (and more understandably) identified as gnostic than any of Dick's other fiction—seems quite unorthodox. The novel was written in 1978, and a survey of *Exegesis* entries from around this time shows a frequent occurrence of references to gnosticism and the Nag Hammadi library. But references to these ideas tapered off over the next few years, reaching a low point toward the end of Dick's life. In their place were references to Greek philosophy—mostly Platonic and pre-Socratic—and to Christian thinkers such as St. Paul, Pierre Teilhard de Chardin, and St. Augustine. One impetus for this transition was a powerful experience on November 17, 1980 (which Dick referred to in the *Exegesis* as "the 11-17-80 theophany," or simply "11-17-80")—a vividly Christian experience which will be discussed further in the next chapter. After this "theophany," Dick rejected, at least temporarily, the *Exegesis* as a whole: "Thus my exegesis has been futile, has been delusion, &: has been a hell-chore... I was at last led to God. But not by my intellect, not by Gnosis, not by myself at all; it was due to God's initiative due to his loving-kindness."[31] After 11-17-80, Dick seems to have been unable to accept those parts of the *Exegesis* that

---

[30] Tessa B. Dick, "Letter to The Philip K. Dick Society." PKDS 17 (April 1988), 12.
[31] Dick, *In Pursuit of Valis*, 54-55.

were not Christian—especially those that expressed the Gnostic belief in an evil demiurge as creator of this world. Even before this Christianity had been near-omnipresent in the *Exegesis*, as Jay Kinney, one of the first individuals to survey the journal as a whole, explains: "While Phil entertained at various times many far-fetched explanations for the 'pink beam' experiences, he consistently returned to Christian theology and Greek philosophy for his most serious interpretations."[32] Christian themes, always present in Dick's religious thought but often upstaged by more heretical speculations, were finally brought to the fore in the *Exegesis*, and rank among the most serious and most fascinating of Dick's theological explorations. Ultimately, Christianity is not a *theory* like the other systems considered in the *Exegesis*, but rather an *assumption*, just like the 2-3-74 experience itself: it is one of the standards to which Dick held up his theories, and if they did not match it, he rejected them.

DEFINING "HUMAN": PAUL FOR THE FUTURE

In a 1974 letter, Dick declared that "I can actually obtain a certain true knowledge of [God] myself by direct study of the Scriptures. It is not up to one human to tell another with a spurious sense of absolute knowledge what God is or says or wishes; we are to go individually directly to the Scriptures, which alone are the authentic source."[33] Dick seems to have eventually become something of an expert on the Bible, and especially on the New Testament: Tessa Dick claimed that "Phil was a Pauline scholar... [he] could hold his own against most priests, in a theological debate."[34] It is likely that Dick felt a certain affinity with Paul after 2-3-74, given the nature of Paul's conversion experience as described in the Book of Acts: "Now as [Saul] was going along and approaching Damascus, suddenly a light from heaven flashed around him. He fell to the ground and heard a voice saying to him, 'Saul, Saul, why do you persecute me?'... Saul got up from the ground, and though his eyes were open, he could see nothing" (Acts 9:3-8). The

---

[32] Jay Kinney, "Summary of the Exegesis," PKDS 3 (1984), 13.
[33] Dick, *Selected Letters: 1974*, 133.
[34] Tessa B. Dick, Letter to PKDS," PKDS 17 (April 1988), 12.

similarity to Dick's experience of the "pink beam" that temporarily blinded him is striking, and Dick drew the comparison himself frequently. He was also fascinated with the idea that Paul was never able to fully communicate what, exactly, he had experienced in his conversion, just as Dick's *Exegesis* can only partially communicate the power of his experience. Dick stated in a 1982 interview: "I saw things. . . that I've never been able to tell anybody. . . and it was like Paul on the road to Damascus when the light hit him and he could never tell people everything."[35] In addition to the literal blinding in both Paul's conversion story and Dick's "pink beam" experiences, there is also a metaphorical blinding, an inability to fully comprehend or communicate the nature of the religious experience. The escapee from Plato's cave is blinded and dazzled by the abundance of light outside of his prison—just so were both Paul and Dick unable to fully grasp the nature of their experiences, and hence unable to explain them fully. Dick definitely drew comfort from the story of Paul following 2-3-74, but his fascination with Paul's life and writings began long before that.

Dick's earlier fondness for Paul's life and ideas is illustrated by the plot of the 1970 novel *Our Friends From Frolix 8*. The novel depicts a future police state in which super-intelligent, autocratic "New Men" hold absolute power over unevolved "Old Men." Several years before the beginning of the novel's action, a man named Thors Provoni had left for another solar system, looking for extraterrestrial assistance in overthrowing the Earth's corrupt government. Provoni has become a beacon of hope for the Old Men, though many do not believe he will return. Eric Cordon, leader of a revolutionary movement called the "Under Men," keeps faith in his mission alive. Cordon announces Provoni's eventual return "in endless speeches, books and grubby tracts" that are distributed among the Under Men until Cordon is executed by the repressive government.[36] This execution does nothing to prevent the Old Men from believing in Provoni's return; before the execution one government official rightly predicts that the people will persistently hold "the belief that Cordon is dead, but that Provoni is not; that he's alive and will return. Even without Cordon. . . thousands [of]—authentic or forged—

---

[35] Gwen Lee and Doris Elaine Sauter. *What If Our World Is Their Heaven? The Final Conversations of Philip K. Dick*. Woodstock and New York: The Overlook Press, 2000, 149.

[36] Dick, *Our Friends From Frolix 8*. New York: Ace Publishing Corporation, 1970, 22 (§4).

writings by Cordon are being circulated everywhere on Earth every minute of the day. His death isn't going to end that."[37] Shortly after Cordon's execution Provoni returns and, with the assistance of a nonviolent alien being, defeats the police state.

The parallel to Jesus and Paul in *Our Friends From Frolix 8* is clear. Provoni's quest for extraterrestrial help echoes Christ's announcement of the Kingdom prior to his Ascension. Cordon's letters and speeches predict Provoni's triumphant return just as Paul's letters reassured the early Christians that "the Lord himself, with a cry of command, with the archangel's call and with the sound of God's trumpet, will descend from heaven" (1 Thess 4:16). Provoni is an allegorical Messiah, gone for a time but soon to return with the power to bring his believers to freedom. Cordon, like Paul, carries this salvific message to the community of believers.

This allegorical representation is by no means the only reference to Paul in all of Dick's writing. Dick's characters quote Paul quite often in conversation, frequently making reference to the ideal of love—*caritas* or *agape*—described in 1 Corinthians. Dick seems to have drawn his definition of humanity, based on the principle of compassion, from Paul's writings. In *The Transmigration of Timothy Archer*, the title character quotes from 1 Corinthians, then further explains the quotation: "You find your place in the world out of love, not animosity. Love is not limited to the Christian, love is not just for the church. If you wish to conquer us, show us love and not scorn. Faith moves mountains, love moves human hearts. The people opposing you are people, not things."[38] Though a fictional character speaks these words, there is little doubt that Dick believed them himself. In numerous interviews he has referred to the act of kindness—no matter how small—as the ultimate expression of true humanity, because it shows a selfless love for one's fellow human beings. This act of kindness goes beyond any other religious experience in spiritual importance, as Dick, paraphrasing Jan van Ruysbroeck, states in a 1982 interview: "If you are ravished in ecstasy as highly as St. Peter or St. Paul, or as anybody you like, and if you hear the sick man is in need of hot soup I counsel you to wake up from your ecstasy and warm the soup for him. Leave God to serve God."[39] This view reflects Paul's exhortation to love in 1 Corinthians, chapter 13,

---

[37] Dick, *Our Friends From Frolix 8*, 49-50 (§8).
[38] Philip K. Dick, *The Transmigration of Timothy Archer.* 1982; rpt. New York: Vintage/Random House, 1991, 31 (§2).
[39] Rickman, *Last Testament*, 133.

arguably the philosophical center of all of Dick's discussion of humanity and certainly the most-cited biblical passage in all of Dick's writing: "If I have prophetic powers, and understand all mysteries and all knowledge, and if I have all faith, so as to remove mountains, but do not have love, I am nothing" (1 Cor 13:2).

Much of Dick's religious and ethical writing can be seen as reinterpreting the Pauline message of selfless love for the future. By placing Paul's beliefs in a futuristic, science-fictional setting, Dick attempts to show how the ideal of love can be realized in a world increasingly controlled by machines. In a 1972 speech delivered at a Vancouver science fiction convention, Dick writes:

> "We see as through a glass darkly," Paul in 1 Corinthians—will this someday be rewritten as, "We see as into a passive infrared scanner darkly?" A scanner that as in Orwell's *1984*, is watching us all the time? Our TV tube watching back at us as we watch it, as amused, or bored, or anyhow somewhat as entertained by what we do as we are by what we see on its implacable face?
>
> This, for me, is too pessimistic, too paranoid. I believe 1 Corinthians will be rewritten this way: "The passive infrared scanner sees into *us* darkly"—that is, not well enough really to figure us out.[40]

This passage presages the title of Dick's 1977 novel *A Scanner Darkly*, a novel that explores the division between the android mind—the reflex machine—and the authentic, caring human being. For Dick, the Pauline ideal of love is and always will be relevant, and he wanted to be certain that loving humanity, rather than android pragmatism, be the human race's ideal. Dick wished to show that Paul's moral vision was still applicable in an age of automation and atomic weapons, as Patricia Warrick explains: "The late twentieth century is a time at war with itself, not with an external enemy. To fight against what one abhors without realizing it lies within is to destroy all."[41] The ideal of love is necessary not only in matters of war and peace, but also in everyday life and scientific advances. In the 1972 Vancouver speech, Dick explains further: "Maybe we should scrutinize more closely the two-legged entities we plan to send up, for example, to the orbiting

---

[40] Dick, "The Android and the Human." In Sutin, ed., *Shifting Realities*, 208.
[41] Patricia Warrick, *Mind in Motion: The Fiction of Philip K. Dick*. Carbondale, Illinois: Southern Illinois University Press, 1987, 195.

space station... [Inside the android] there is a vacuum. A place unfilled. The *absence* of something vital—that is the horrific part, the apocalyptic vision of a nightmare future."[42] Dick saw Paul's ideal of love as the solution to the potential ethical dilemmas of the technological future, and much of his science fiction may be read as futurological interpretations of that ideal.

TRUTH DIVIDED: DICK AND THE LOGOS

Dick's interest in Scripture did not begin and end with Paul. His writing makes frequent reference to the Gospel of John, in particular the prologue's statement that "In the beginning was the Word, and the Word was with God, and the Word was God" (Jn 1:1). The concept of Christ as a living Word fascinated Dick, and much of his writing refers to the doctrine of *logos* developed in early Christianity. Like all of his ideas, Dick's conception of the *logos* underwent a number of changes, because, as Warrick states, "for him the Word was truly the Living Word, the power that creates and re-creates patterns. Trapped in the stasis of a final statement, the Word would have been defeated by entropy and death."[43] But his thoughts on the *logos* always remained engaging interpretations of Christian doctrine, and he consistently identified *logos*—whether he thought of it as the primordial Word, the hidden message of salvation, or an extraterrestrial form of living information—with Christ.

Dick's ideas about the *logos*, which form a significant portion of the *Exegesis*, are linked to the Christian concept, articulated by Augustine, that Scripture is complete; that is, that it contains only truth, and that every truth is contained in it:

> A spring enclosed in a narrow space is more abundant and pours its flow by more streams over a wider countryside than any single one of those same streams however long its course. Similarly the writing of the dispenser of Your word, since it was meant to be of service to many who later should preach upon it, sets flowing in its brevity of utterance torrents of clear truth from which each may draw such truth as he can, one man this, another that, but with far lengthier windings of words.[44]

---

[42] Dick, "The Android and the Human." In Sutin, ed., *Shifting Realities*, 190.

[43] Warrick, *Mind in Motion*, 194.

[44] St. Augustine, St. *Confessions, Books I-XIII*, trans. F.J. Sheed. Indianapolis/

Thus, for Augustine, Scripture—the temporal *logos* that reflects God's creative and sustaining Word—is a finite source from which infinite truth springs. Since, for Augustine, Scripture contains all truths, it is possible to speak truthfully at all times using only the words of the Bible. Augustine's hope was to gradually replace his human, world-oriented words with the constant remembrance and praise of God: "If only I only spoke when preaching your word and praising you! . . . Deliver me, my God, from the much speaking which I suffer from inwardly in my soul."[45] The *logos* is thus transformative—it can reshape the individual and make his or her mind a true image of God. For Augustine, *logos* was the temporally limited source of limitless truth, but also the power by which humanity could discover and actualize God's will.

In *The Divine Invasion*, Dick expresses a very similar concept in science-fictional terms. The novel describes a holographic representation of the entire Bible; a brilliantly colored light-sculpture representing the entire Christian canon. This device allows the viewer to see the entirety of Scripture at once, as it is represented as "a three-dimensional cosmos that could be viewed from any angle and its contents read. According to the tilt of the axis of observation, differing messages could be extracted. Thus Scripture yielded up an infinitude of knowledge that ceaselessly changed."[46] This description is a remarkable SF parallel to Augustine's spring of truth, and demonstrates Dick's belief in the authority of Christian Scripture, his conviction, expressed in a letter quoted above, that he could gain knowledge of God through direct study of Scripture.

Dick also articulated a number of different views of the *logos* and its operation in our world. Perhaps foremost among these ideas is the concept that the temporal form of the *logos* itself is piecemeal, scattered throughout every word ever written or spoken. This concept is described on an audio tape of notes Dick made in 1974 for a proposed sequel to his novel *The*

Cambridge: Hackett, 1993, 252-253 (12:27). In the *Exegesis* excerpts published to date, Dick does not refer to Augustine specifically on the matter of the *logos*. But Dick was undoubtedly familiar with Augustine's writings, and he elsewhere refers to concepts laid out in *On the Trinity*, *The City of God*, and *The Confessions*. It is likely, then, that Dick was familiar with Augustine's formulation of this concept of the completeness of Scripture.

[45] St. Augustine, *The Trinity*, trans. Edmund Hill, O.P., ed. John E. Rotell, O.S.A. Brooklyn, New York: New City Press, 1991, 436 (15:51).

[46] Dick, *The Divine Invasion*, 70 (§6).

Man in the High Castle. These recorded notes eventually grew into the handwritten *Exegesis*, and the proposed novel became an early draft for what eventually became *VALIS*. In these notes, he states the idea that *every* word is potentially part of a divine message:

> [The] transduction system is built from two halves: one in his head, one outside. The one outside is all the *logos* that comes to him, all the written things, every piece of written thing, on TV, magazines, newspapers, books—anything written down. . . This all works by a coupling of parts, each fragment of which appears as a whole, a gestalt, like "Eat whole wheat bread." That's a complete sentence, and it never occurs to you that it might be a portion of another message. It is a portion that, when added to another thing that is a complete message, forms. . . an entirely different message and not a debased one. It is out of these debased molecules of trash that the messages come.[47]

Dick's concept of messages from "debased molecules of trash" is closely connected to his overall theology: the idea, to be discussed in more detail in the next chapter, that God is hidden in the world and reveals Himself where He is least expected. Based on this concept, Dick searched for the piecemeal logos everywhere: in television commercials, popular music, Greek philosophy and—perhaps most importantly—in his own stories and novels. Significant portions of the *Exegesis* are made up of explorations and interpretations of Dick's work, for reasons he explains in a 1977 entry: "No one book or story is correct & the others incorrect, & no one book or story tells it *all*. Many of them must be read."[48] Dick picked his own books apart searching for scraps of truth, and found it in many places—though what those truths were shifted from day to day, or even hour to hour. The truth, he also felt, could be found in a broad variety of places in human history, as a 1980 *Exegesis* entry explains: "The truth—like the self—is splintered up over

---

[47] Philip K. Dick, "Notes for Work in Progress, Circa August 1974." PKDS 9/10 (January 1986, audio cassette). The notes begin by referring to Hawthorne Abendsen (the "he" of the first sentence in this quotation), a character in *The Man in the High Castle* on whom the sequel was to be centered. But the experiences Dick describes the character undergoing are identical to some of the experiences of 2-3-74, and the character eventually became Nicholas Brady in *Radio Free Albemuth* and Horselover Fat in *VALIS*. Later in the recorded notes, Dick seems to forget the planned novel completely, and begins simply exploring theories for their own sake. Though these notes were for a fictional story, the philosophical themes and the experiences that engender them are autobiographical.

[48] Dick, *In Pursuit of Valis*, 167.

thousands of miles and years; bits are found here and there, then and now, and must be re-collected; bits appear in Greek naturalists, in Pythagoras, in Plato, Parmenides, in Heraclitus, Neo-Platonism, Zoroastrianism, Gnosticism, Taoism... Each religion or philosophy or philosopher contains one or more bits, but the total system interweaves it into falsity."[49] Only when the pieces of truth are separated and connected to one another does a consistent, true system begin to take shape.

Dick's early idea of the piecemeal *logos* is an interesting adaptation of the Augustinian notion of the completeness of Scripture. For Augustine and many other Christian thinkers, Scripture alone is the "spring of truth"; for Dick, Scripture *is* authoritative, but the *logos* is also to be found scattered throughout the entire history of human language. This infinite *logos* is connected from a wide variety of sources, and unites to become an infinitely powerful force, as described in the notes for the sequel to *The Man in the High Castle*: "His book fits in with somebody else's book, and somebody else's song, and somebody else's letter in the paper, and somebody else's everything... The Nazis are overthrown by the *I Ching*."[50] The *I Ching*, the Gospel of John, bread advertisements and alphabet soup—all of these pieces of writing, for Dick, are connected, linked as a form of communication from a transcendent and benevolent being easily identifiable as God.

As time went on and Dick's *Exegesis* grew, his interpretations of the function of *logos* in the world changed, growing closer to the orthodox Christian doctrine of the Word. Dick read a large number of theological texts, including the works of Philo of Alexandria, a Jewish theologian who was a contemporary of both Jesus and Paul. Though not a Christian himself, Philo's ideas about the nature of God's creative speech in Genesis had a powerful effect on Christian doctrine regarding God's Word. For Philo, "The *logos* was the image of God... [and] also served as the paradigm or model for the ordering of the rest of the universe... It was also the instrument (*organon*) through which the universe was ordered ... and the power by which the universe continued to be ordered."[51] God's creative speech is a continuous act, and the Word sustains the universe it has created. This concept was an epiphany for Dick when he came across it, as one long and energetic *Exegesis* entry shows:

---

[49] Dick, *In Pursuit of Valis*, 111-112.
[50] Dick, "Notes for work in progress." PKDS 9/10 (January 1986, audio cassette).
[51] Thomas H. Tobin, "Logos," in David Noel Freedmen, ed.-in-chief, *The Anchor Bible Dictionary*, vol. 4, New York: Doubleday, 1992, 350.

> To repeat: the abstract structural (nonsubstantial) basis of reality is also the agent of creation of reality, for from it stems that which we term "reality": plural physical objects in space and time, controlled by causal laws. It is this agent of creation that Philo surnamed *Logos* and which we identify with both Christ and Hagia Sophia (the wisdom of God). This is what I say, as total insubstantial abstract structure. . . the abstract structure is not *outside* reality (like potter to pot, artisan to artifact); this insubstantial abstract structure *is* reality properly conceived.[52]

Here Dick, in keeping with the Christian concept of *logos*, identifies the Word as the agent and the plan of creation, as well as Jesus Christ—the Word made flesh. A passage quoted above from Dick's novel *The Divine Invasion* describing the "St. Elmo's Fire" phenomenon shows a similar view of the *logos*. The fiery energy that forms words and pools like blood suggests both the creative, sustaining word and the redemptive blood shed on the cross. Dick describes this energy in several places in his writing, both fiction and non-fiction. The description in *The Divine Invasion* is the most vivid, however, and there it is most clear that he believed "St. Elmo's Fire" to be a vision of the action of the *logos*.

The seed for this understanding can be seen in a 1975 *Exegesis* entry in which Dick states: "I conceive of it [God] as a builder, an artificer, who creates, in conformity to its Plan: the *Logos* (I conceive of *Logos* as a blueprint of something to be actualized)."[53] In addition to being the plan and agent of all existence, *logos* is also the only actual reality; God alone can be said to have real existence. Dick explores this idea further in a 1979 *Exegesis* entry: "The epiphenomenal is real insofar as it partakes of God & only insofar as it does."[54] A 1978 essay directly links this idea to the Cosmic Christ, who is identified with the *logos*: "It is the act of absolute faith: to deny the empirical world and affirm the living reality of Christ, which is to say, Christ with us, hidden by the pseudoworld. This disclosure is the ultimate goal of authentic Christianity, and it is accomplished by none other than the Savior Himself."[55] As Dick moved toward this later summation of the *logos* as plan and agent of creation and Christ as the only true possessor of being, his view came quite close to Christian orthodoxy.

---

[52] Dick, *In Pursuit of Valis*, 126-127.
[53] Dick, *In Pursuit of Valis*, 67.
[54] Dick, *In Pursuit of Valis*, 44.
[55] Dick, "Cosmogony and Cosmology." In Sutin, ed., *Shifting Realities*, 289.

Dick had long held the belief that the *logos* was individually transformative, a view voiced by Augustine: "For you have already been made through the Word, but it is necessary that you be remade through the Word... And if it has fallen to your lot to be made through the Word, so that through it you were made, through yourself you are defective. If you are defective through yourself, it is necessary that the One who has made you should remake you."[56] Dick felt transformed by the 2-3-74 experience in a very literal way: as discussed above, he believed himself to have been taken over by another person or entity. His very manner of looking at the world around him was altered, as he describes in a 1974 letter: "I saw in a deeply religious fashion: actually, I traced out with my eyes as I walked to the store the presence of God here and there, and understood all sorts of things about the vast and active process of continual creation. For me it was a new world, a fresh one."[57] Dick felt that he had been transformed by the *logos*, the activity of which he was then able to see as it transformed, sustained, and created the world. He was able to observe the action of the *logos* in the world only after it had transformed him, and this observation—seeing the world as it really is—was the end result of this transformation.

Dick science-fictionalized the concept of *logos* in his novel *VALIS*, in which Horselover Fat theorizes that the universe is in fact made of information inside the mind of God: "Thoughts of the brain are experienced by us as arrangements and rearrangements—change—in a physical universe, but in fact it is really information and information-processing which we substantialize... The linking and relinking of objects by the Brain is actually a language."[58] Further, Fat posits a being composed of pure information that can bond with individual humans in a form of religious experience: "I term the Immortal one a *plasmate*, because it is a form of energy; it is living information. It replicates itself—not through information or in information—but as information... As living information, the plasmate travels up the optic nerve of a human to the pineal body. It uses the human brain as a female host in which to replicate itself into its active form. This is an interspecies symbiosis."[59] This seemingly outlandish theory can be read

---

[56] St. Augustine, "First Homily on the Gospel of St. John." 12. In *Augustine of Hippo: Selected Writings,* Trans. and ed. Mary T. Clark. New York: Paulist Press, 1984, 274-275 (12).
[57] Dick, *Selected Letters: 1974,* 216.
[58] Dick, *VALIS,* 234 (Appendix).
[59] Dick, *VALIS,* 231-232 (Appendix).

as an allegorical explanation of the *logos* doctrine in science-fictional terms, as Dick's religious theories channeled through the mind of the fictional Fat. The extraterrestrial plasmate—which lies dormant in esoteric religious texts until "awakened" by a reader—fulfills the transformative function of the *logos*. The transformation of perspective brought about by the *logos* is depicted as a symbiotic relationship in which the living Word gradually reconstructs the individual, shaping him or her in such a manner that he or she can perceive the absolute reality underlying the phenomenal world. For Dick, the two functions of the *logos*—continual creation and individual transformation—were intimately linked, and he consistently identified God's Word with Jesus Christ.

THE CENTRALITY OF CHRIST IN DICK'S RELIGIOUS WRITING

Despite the ever-shifting nature of Dick's cosmological theories, Christ is absolutely central throughout all of his religious speculations. In books, essays, interviews, and *Exegesis* entries, Dick constantly referred to Christ, the *logos*, the Holy Spirit, and countless other key Christian concepts. Can he thus be identified as a Christian thinker? Many of the gnostics with whom Dick is often identified by scholars and fans also believed Christ to be the Savior, used the writings of Paul, and accepted the doctrine of the *logos*—what, in these concepts, separates Dick from these more strictly dualistic sects of early Christianity?

Dick was not a "Gnostic," but this is not because he believed in Christ—he was Christian because, despite much extravagant theorizing, he was unable to accept gnostic dualism itself. In an *Exegesis* entry quoted above, Dick directly denounced the Manichean view, taken form Gnostic concepts, that the world of creation is evil, and a similar passage from 1975 further shows this anti-gnostic theme: "God. . . takes no pleasure in the destruction of any living thing: he created all things that they might have being. The creative forces of the world make for life; there are no deadly poisons in them. Death is not King on Earth, for Justice is immortal."[60] Evil is an illusion, and the only true reality belongs to God. Dualism is a veil that conceals the fact that God underlies all existence. In a 1976 speech, Dick explains a dualistic theory that is actually monistic, a theory that describes the universe as a chess game God plays against himself:

---

[60] Dick, *In Pursuit of Valis*, 249.

Underlying the two game players there is God, who is neither and both. The effect of the game is that both players become purified. Thus the ancient Hebrew monotheism, so superior to our own view. We are creatures in a game with our affinities and aversions predetermined for us—not by blind chance but by patient, foresighted engramming systems that we dimly see. Were we to see them clearly, we would abolish the game. Evidently that would not serve anyone's interests.[61]

In *Radio Free Albemuth*, an early version of *VALIS* so different from the final novel that it was posthumously published as a separate novel, one character offers a very similar theory, further emphasizing the ultimate goodness of both "players": "No matter how much they might seem to conflict or work against each other, they commonly desired the successful outcome of their joint enterprise. . . these twin entities were manifestations of a single substance."[62] One of the key tenets of many of the gnostic systems—in particular of Manicheism—is the belief that evil is real, that it contains tangible existence. This was a concept that Dick repeatedly and emphatically rejected, despite his frequent theorizing on the illusory nature of this world. In the end, he believed this world to be unreal not because it was *evil* or created by an evil deity, but because it is *good*, and a benevolent, omnipresent deity underlies it. This deity is in the process of improving the world, as Dick describes in his 1974 notes: "Something lies ahead. Something lies past the suffering on the other side; it's as simple as that. It doesn't make suffering good, but there's something beyond it. He looks—his gaze is fastened on that. He's able to fix his gaze away from the suffering. He sees the Spirit using everything. Fashioning amongst all the pieces around him and in the world the growing structure of the new."[63] This Spirit is not in opposition to an evil deity—it is merely reshaping its own substance according to its *logos*, its plan of itself. The God Dick believed in was the Christian God, and it was Christianity to which his theories ultimately returned.

---

[61] Dick, "Man, Android, and Machine." In Sutin, ed., *Shifting Realities*, 214.
[62] Dick, *Radio Free Albemuth.* 1985; rpt. New York: Vintage/Random House, 1998, 122 (§18).
[63] Dick, "Notes for work-in-progress." PKDS 9/10 (January 1986, audio cassette).

CHAPTER THREE:

Infinity, Play Again:
The Nature and Importance of
Dick's Religious Speculations

I think that in 3-74, at the height of despair and fear and grieving I stumbled into the Kingdom, stumbled around for a while and then stumbled back out, none the wiser as to how I got there, barely aware of where I had been, and no idea as to how I stumbled out, and seeking always to find my way back ever since. Shucks. Drat.
—Exegesis entry, 1975[1]

You know how I am with theories. Theories are like planes at LA International: a new one along every minute.
—Radio Free Albemuth[2]

Truly, you are a God who hides himself, O God of Israel, the Savior.
—Isaiah 45:15

BEYOND INFINITY:
THE THEORETICAL NATURE OF DICK'S RELIGIOUS THOUGHT

2-3-74 was a mystery for Philip K. Dick. He knew that he had experienced something, but despite eight years of *Exegesis*-writing, discussion, and even new experiences, he was unable to make a final statement regarding the source and meaning of his encounter. All he could do was devise theories in a desperate attempt to understand 2-3-74, to place it into a context in which everything made sense. In *VALIS*, narrator-Phil despairs of this situation:

---
[1] Dick, *In Pursuit of Valis*, 31-32.
[2] Dick, *Radio Free Albemuth*, 139 (§19).

"During the years—outright years!—that he labored on his exegesis, Fat must have come up with more theories than there are stars in the universe. Every day he developed a new one, more cunning, more exciting and more fucked."[3] At the core of Dick's religious thought are theories to be tested and rejected, not statements of faith. The *Exegesis* contains both accounts of experience and analyses of their possible meaning, but the line between the two is so thin as to be nearly nonexistent. Each time Dick recorded an experience, he interpreted it through the framework of a particular theory, shifting the hypothesis to fit the facts of the actual event and playing up certain aspects of the event to make it fit the theory. His goal was to fully comprehend his experience, as Warrick writes: "His goal . . .is to do more than rejoice in revelation; he wishes to understand it. He insists that the theophany experienced by the mystic must be comprehended before it can be accepted."[4] Having "stumbled into the Kingdom," Dick wanted to find out just what the Kingdom was.

The variety of Dick's experiences in 2-3-74 made it very difficult for him to find a theory that fit, however. No one framework seemed to be able to account for all of the facts regarding his encounter. In a 1977 interview, Dick explains: "I['ve] got this jar in my head of facts that don't fit any theory. You know, there's 3,000 theories, but the jar stays full with a constant amount of facts. Some get taken out, but every time one's taken out, another one's got to go back in."[5] It is these unexplainable facts that kept Dick from ever settling on one theory. If he had been able to develop a hypothesis that accounted for all of the facts in the "jar," his *Exegesis*, and his religious experience, would have been complete: he would have discovered the Answer. Instead, he was left to think and rethink his hypotheses, as he states in a 1975 interview: "On Thursdays and Saturdays I would think it was God, on Tuesdays and Wednesdays I would think it was extraterrestrial, sometimes I would think it was the Soviet Academy of Sciences trying out their psychotronic microwave telepathic transmitter."[6] Dick did not simply change between theories, however—very often he would reject old hypotheses outright. In a 1981 interview, he explains this aspect of the theorizing process: "I . . . get different thoughts that come to me and I'll work on them for half an hour or

---

[3] Dick, *VALIS*, 32 (§3).
[4] Warrick, "Dick's Answers." In Reilly, ed., *The Transcendent Adventure*, 123.
[5] Apel, *The Dream Connection*, 80.
[6] Platt, *Dream Makers*, 155.

a couple days and then discard them. Like I work on almost a kind of random basis. You know I'll try a heuristic (self-learning) process on my part. I'll try every different idea and drop those that don't work and then go to the ones that do... [After coming up with a new idea,] I'm going to work on that idea for a couple days and I'll probably discard it as not workable."[7] This process could take as long as a few months, as in the period of extensive speculation on gnosticism and the Nag Hammadi texts, or a matter of minutes, as in numerous interviews. Because Dick threw himself into each new theory with energy, fervor and conviction, he needed to discount old hypotheses in order to move on to new ones. Rejection of ideas is a definitive aspect of Dick's process of theory-making.

This periodic rejection of old ideas might make Dick's inability to settle on any ideas seem a weakness in his religious writing. In *VALIS*, narrator-Phil comments derisively on Fat's theories, characterizing them as blind attempts at giving meaning to an essentially meaningless experience. In *The Transmigration of Timothy Archer*, Angel Archer believes the title character suffers from the same problem: "he could believe in anything and he would immediately act on the basis of his new belief; that is, until he ran into another belief and then he acted on that... [He] believed everything he saw written down."[8] This mindset leads ultimately to Tim's death, as he focuses more on his theories than on the necessities of life. Dick sometimes adapted a similarly cynical attitude to his theorizing, as in a 1974 letter:

> My colloquy with the spirit or sibyl runs sort of like this:
> PKD: Who and what are you?
> S: I know what is going on. (Holds up book)
> PKD: Fuck that—I want to know where you come from and—
> S: Here's a couple of Sanskrit words to satisfy you that I know everything. Vis, lig, ir, leg. Look them up and check. (Shows)
> PKD: (hours, days later): Amazing. How did—
> S: Your society is in danger. Your counterintelligence people know about it but can't say anything. Terrorists of a religious, fanatical sort will soon—
> PKD (interrupting excitedly) You know anything about the Orphic doctrine of reincarnation? The triparte [sic] divisions of the afterlife derived from—(Drones on. Spirit exit. Omnia exeunt)[9]

---

[7] Rickman, *Last Testament*, 112.
[8] Dick, *The Transmigration of Timothy Archer*, 17-18 (§2).
[9] Dick, *Selected Letters: 1974*, 171.

Dick occasionally feared that his constant theorizing might cover up the truth about his experience, rather than revealing it. At other times, he felt that his theories were too complex to be possible, and he even despaired of understanding his ideas himself. In a 1982 interview, Dick explains: "My problem arose when [I] picked up some of these things and started reading them over and they were too difficult for me to read over. I could invent them, but I couldn't understand them after I'd invented them."[10] Dick occasionally feared that his constant analysis of his experience would ultimately veil from him the truth that he sought.

But these cynical moments are rare in the *Exegesis*, and Dick more frequently implied that the act of creating new theories was vital to his religious experience. Regardless of factual truth or falsity, he believed that every line of thought regarding his experience could lead to valuable insights. In a 1977 *Exegesis* entry, he writes: "'Actualities are somehow plucked from a greater sea of possibilities that also form part of the truth.' This means that the actuality is not true versus possibilities that are false; it just means that the actuality is more true; the possibilities are less true but also true... It is a question of degree, not either-or."[11] Dick's constant theorizing points to his belief that truth is a matter not of actuality, but of probability—in such a system, a hypothesis is of equal value to a statement of fact. "Truth" cannot be limited to factual statements alone. In his 1974 notes for an early draft of *VALIS*, Dick further expresses this idea in an explanation of his main character's quest: "Every theory works... Everything that's ever been said about it is true. It's always honest... He applies a hundred different theories as to what happened to him... and everything seems to apply, all seems to be true."[12] Dick regarded the theoretical process of the *Exegesis* as a game, an eternal and unsolvable puzzle the goal of which was to create an infinitude of theories regarding the source and meaning of his experience.

This idea reached its ultimate expression late in November 1980, in what Dick referred to as his "11-17-80 theophany." The experience was arguably as important to Dick as 2-3-74 itself, and it revitalized his efforts to explore his religious experiences. Perhaps most importantly, it emphasized

---

[10] Lee and Sauter, *What If Our World Is Their Heaven*, 82.
[11] Dick, "Selections from the *Exegesis*." In Sutin, ed., *Shifting Realities*, 329.
[12] Dick, "Notes for a work-in-progress," PKDS 9/10 (January 1986, audio cassette).

the importance of continued theorization. Dick wrote a long *Exegesis* entry immediately following the events of 11-17-80 in which he recounted the experience as a dialogue:

> God manifested himself to me as the infinite void; but it was not the abyss; it was the vault of heaven, with blue sky and wisps of white clouds. He was not some foreign God but the God of my fathers. He was loving and kind and he had personality. He said, "You suffer a little now in life, it is little compared with the great joys, the bliss that awaits you. Do you think I in my theodicy would allow you to suffer greatly in proportion to your reward?" He made me aware, then, of the bliss that would come; it was infinite and sweet.[13]

This passage indicates that Dick came to believe that the source of his revelations was the Christian God. The references to the vault of heaven, the God of his ancestors, and the eternal "bliss that would come" all stand in stark contrast to Dick's earlier, gnostic speculations regarding a dualistic cosmology and an evil demiurge, as well as contradicting his more "secular" theories that his experience originated with extraterrestrials or Soviet science experiments. Dick emphasizes the ontological unity of God:

> He said, "I am the infinite. I will show you. Where I am, infinity is; where infinity is, there I am. Construct lines of reasoning by which to understand you experience in 1974. I will enter the field against their shifting nature. You think they are logical but they are not; they are infinitely creative."[14]

God—or what Dick experienced as God—here emphasizes the theoretical basis of Dick's religious speculation. This seems a response to Dick's despair over the fact that, despite years of writing the *Exegesis*, his theories had brought him no closer to a final conclusion regarding the origin of his experience. God "enters the field," guaranteeing that the apparently aimless process of theorization is not useless:

> I thought a thought and then an infinite regression of theses and countertheses came into being. God said, "Here I am, here is infinity." I thought another explanation; again an infinite series of thoughts split off in a dialectical antithetical interaction. God said, "Here is infinity; here I am." I thought, then, an infinite number of explanations, in succession, that explained 2-3-74; each single

---

[13] Dick, *In Pursuit of Valis*, 45.
[14] Dick, *In Pursuit of Valis*, 45.

one of them yielded up an infinite progression of flipflops, of thesis and antithesis, forever. Each time, God said "Here is infinity. Here, then, I am." I tried for an infinite number of times; each time and infinite regress was set off and each time God said, "Infinity. Hence I am here." Then he said, "Every thought leads to infinity, does it not? Find one that doesn't." I tried forever. All led to an infinitude of regress, of the dialectic, of thesis, antithesis and new synthesis. Each time, God said "Here is infinity; here am I. Try again." I tried forever. Always it ended with God saying, "Infinity and myself, I am here." I saw, then, a Hebrew letter with many shafts, and all the shafts led to a common outlet; that outlet or conclusion was infinity. God said, "That is myself. I am infinity. Where infinity is, there am I; where I am, there is infinity. All roads—all explanations for 2-3-74—lead to an infinity of Yes-No, This or That, On-Off, One-Zero, Yin-Yang, the dialectic, infinity upon infinity; an infinities [*sic*] of infinities. I am everywhere and all roads lead to me; *omnia viae ad Deum ducent* [*all roads lead to God*]. Try again. Think of another possible explanation for 2-3-74." I did; it led to an infinity of regress, of thesis and antithesis and new synthesis. "This is not logic," God said.[15]

Dick's theories, since they ultimately could not be verified, could only lead to more theories. But in the 11-17-80 theophany, Dick realized that this "infinite regress" was in fact an example of the divine presence in the world. His process was not fruitless or insane; rather, like all things, it was an example of the presence of infinity in the world, the in-breaking of eternity into our temporal realm. God further attempts to prove that he is the source of both 2-3-74 and the *Exegesis* that followed it, appealing not to dualistic, yes-no logic, but rather to "probabilities":

"Do not think in terms of absolute theories; think instead in term of probabilities. Watch where the piles heap up, of the same theory essentially repeating itself. Count the number of punch cards in each pile. Which pile is highest? You can never know for sure what 2-3-74 was. What, then, is statistically most probable? Which is to say, which pile is highest? Here is your clue: every theory leads to an infinity (of regression, of thesis and antithesis and new synthesis). What, then, is the probability that I am the cause of 2-3-74, since, where infinity is, there I am? . . . Do not try to know; you cannot know. Guess on the basis of the highest pile of computer punch cards. There is an infinite stack in the heap marked INFINITY, and I have equated infinity with me. What,

---

[15] Dick, *In Pursuit of Valis*, 45-46.

then, is the chance that it is me? You cannot be positive; you will doubt. But what is your guess?"

I said, "Probably it is you, since there is an infinity of infinities forming before me."

"There is the answer, the only one you will ever have," God said.

"You could be pretending to be God," I said, "and actually be Satan." Another infinitude of thesis and antithesis and new synthesis, the infinite regress, was set off.

God said, "Infinity."

I said, "You could be testing out a logic system in a giant computer and I am—" Again an infinite regress.

"Infinity," God said.

"Will it always be infinite?" I said. "An infinity?"

"Try further," God said.

"I doubt if you exist," I said. And the infinite regress instantly flew into motion once more.

"Infinity," God said. The pile of computer punch cards grew; it was by far the largest pile; it was infinite.

"I will play this game forever," God said, "or until you become tired."[16]

This image of "computer punch cards" containing Dick's endless theories is perhaps the most striking image in the entire *Exegesis*, as well as an accurate symbol for the work as a whole. It is further a symbol of God as a game-player, and revelation as a benevolent sort of trick. The purpose of the revelation, this passage suggests, was simply to cause Dick to come up with an infinite number of theories, but this is not so that he wastes his time searching for an answer he cannot find. Rather, it is so that he may become an instrument of God's action in our world, the "divine invasion" of the infinite into the finite. Dick devoted himself to playing this game:

I said, "I will find a thought, an explanation, a theory, that does not set off an infinite regress." And, as soon as I said that, an infinite regress was set off. God said "Over a period of six and a half years you have developed theory after theory to explain 2-3-74. Each night when you go to bed you think, 'At last I found it. I tried out theory after theory until now, finally, I have the right one.' And then the next morning you wake up and say, 'There is one fact not explained by that theory. I will have to think up another theory.' And so you do. By now it is evident to you that you are going to think up an infinite number of theories, limited only by

---

[16] Dick, *In Pursuit of Valis*, 46–47.

your lifespan, not limited by your creative imagination. Each theory gives rise to a subsequent theory, inevitably... And your theories are infinite, so I am there. Without realizing it, the very infinitude of your theories pointed to the solution; they pointed to me and none but me... Do I change, or do your theories change?"

"You do not change," I said. "My theories change. You, and 2-3-74, remain constant... This is my punishment," I said, "that I play, that I try to discern if it was you in March of 1974." And the thought came instantly, My punishment or my reward; which? And an infinite series of thesis and antithesis was set off.

"Infinity," God said. "Play again. I am waiting."[17]

The *Exegesis* was merely a game that Dick played with God. The goal of this game was for God to have another place to enter the world, in the endless theorizing of Dick's writing. Dick's conclusion in this passage—that God does not change, but rather only his theories—did not bring the process of theorizing to a halt. Rather, it simply opened a new world of possible theories, and an additional infinitude of places where God might reveal himself. Dick's discussions of the 11-17-80 theophany are perhaps the most important sections of the *Exegesis*, for they reveal some of Dick's most profound thoughts on the nature and meaning of his religious experience as a whole.

The God that Dick experienced creates worlds, but those worlds are games and puzzles. In a speech quoted above, Dick described the universe as a chess game that God plays in order to purify both Himself and His creation. Dick viewed 2-3-74 as an initiation into one of God's games; a glimpse at the purifying play underlying the world that we see. This same view is revealed in the *VALIS* Trilogy. Both *VALIS* and *The Divine Invasion* refer frequently to a fragment of Heraclitus: "Time is a child at play, playing draughts; a child's is the kingdom."[18] Play is essential to the theology of these novels, especially in *The Divine Invasion*, the plot of which centers on a wager between two characters who are in fact the split syzygy of the godhead. At one point in the novel, Emmanuel says, "He [God] enjoys games and play. It says in Scripture that he rested [on the seventh day of creation] but I say that he played."[19] The 11-17-80 experience expands on this theme of God-as-

---

[17] Dick, *In Pursuit of Valis*, 47-51.
[18] Dick, *The Divine Invasion*, 137 (§11). This passage is also quoted elsewhere in the *VALIS* Trilogy.
[19] Dick, *The Divine Invasion*, 73 (§6).

gameplayer, emphasizing the benevolent and purifying nature of the game God plays. Puzzles, paradoxes, and infinite theorizing—all are part of the eternal, benevolent game in which all creation is the board.

PENULTIMATE TRUTH: THE UNREALITY OF THE COSMOS

Underlying experienced existence is God, and God is playing a game. The idea that something lies beneath the world that we see, that the phenomenal universe is a veil concealing the true reality, is absolutely central to nearly all of Dick's metaphysical and religious speculations. The reality-questioning in his novels and stories throughout his career culminated in this conviction, as stated in a 1974 letter: "We cannot go on appearances in life, but must somehow penetrate to the essence, which may be opposite entirely to the phenomenon, the illusion or delusion."[20] Our real state is hidden to us, and is akin to a deep sleep, as Dick writes in a 1975 letter: "We are actually dead now, and lie in graves row on row. Dreaming delusional dreams in our mass graves, these plastic apartments we live in. It is not life; life lies ahead as we recover our senses and wake up."[21] The source and purpose of the "delusional dream" of phenomenal reality is unknown, and is one of the many things about which Dick theorized in the *Exegesis*. Despite this uncertainty, he consistently asserted the opinion that things are not exactly as they appear. Dick drew support for this view from many places, perhaps most importantly from Paul's statement in 1 Corinthians 13:12 that we see "as through a glass, darkly," regarding which Dick said in a 1976 essay: "[Paul] is referring to the familiar notion of Plato's that we see only images of reality, and probably these images are inaccurate and imperfect and not to be relied on. I wish to add that Paul was probably saying one thing more than Plato in the celebrated metaphor of the cave: Paul was saying that we may well be seeing the universe backward."[22] Paul's metaphor is that of a mirror, and a mirror reflects things not as they are but reversed spatially: in a reflection, left and right are switched. Dick's interpretation of Paul's statement concludes that our world is the opposite of how it should be, or at

---

[20] Dick, *Selected Letters: 1974*, 181.
[21] Dick, *Selected Letters: 1975-1976*, 6.
[22] Dick, "Man, Android, and Machine." In Sutin, ed., *Shifting Realities*, 215.

least that we perceive it as the opposite of how it actually is. Dick's writing, both fiction and non-fiction, is filled with the assertion that the world as we perceive it is not real, and with the further conviction that there is a reality that is "more real" underlying the illusions that we perceive.

We cannot see the authentic reality that lies beneath the phenomenal world because we have somehow been separated from it and made incapable of perceiving it. In a 1980 *Exegesis* entry, Dick offers an explanation for this separation: "The theories about the Fall must be revised; an intellectual error, not a moral error, must be presumed. One can almost—almost—view Satan's activity as a high technology in which the simulation of a world order is achieved. . . We fell asleep because we were induced into falling asleep; the spurious world had to be there for us to take it as real."[23] In this system, the Fall of Man is a falling-for-it, mistaking an illusion for reality. The Serpent does not tempt us to sin, but rather he tricks us, deluding us into accepting a false system of order. A 1974 letter explains this further: "What deforms and obscures the actual world is the Lie placed there, inserted between us and God's world by the Master of the Lie, known to Christians as the Prince or Powers of Darkness. . . You must conceive of the Master of the Lie having inserted his realm between us and the true God. Everywhere we look there it is, the Liar and the Lie."[24] This formulation is not as strictly dualistic as it seems: in many places, Dick stated that God underlies both "players"—good and evil—in the cosmic chess-game, and that the Lie may, or even must, serve a greater salvific purpose. The veil between humankind and God exists for the mutual purification of Creator and creation, and this purification depends on the veil's presence so that it may be redemptively lifted.

This illusion can be broken by revelation, which can be defined as authentic reality breaking into the spurious phenomenal world. Revelation is not a distortion or a change in the existing order of the world, but rather a glimpse of the actual nature of existence. Dick explains in a 1975 *Exegesis* entry: "My 3-74 experience—the intervention by God in the world—was not an anomaly, except in terms of my experience of it. That is to say, it was a natural, regular event, which I had just never seen before; however, it always goes on, went on, will go on forever. It is the perpetual re-establishment of equilibrium and harmony."[25] Dick's experience, as he saw it, was simply the

---

[23] Dick, *In Pursuit of Valis*, 111.
[24] Dick, *Selected Letters: 1974*, 187.
[25] Dick, *In Pursuit of Valis*, 25.

perception of God's action in the world, an action that goes on regardless of whether or not it is perceived. This revelation can happen to anyone: in a 1974 letter, Dick states that "I don't feel I was 'picked' by a Future Force, as its instrument, etc., bidden to make manifest its word, etc., anymore than when you are watching a TV program the transmitter has picked you. It is broadcast; it just radiates out in all directions and some people tune in, some do not. . . All I did was to transduce, as all creatures do."[26] Absolute reality is always present and always accessible through the process of revelation, which Dick frequently referred to as "anamnesis"—the loss of amnesia. This idea is drawn from Platonic philosophy, in which the individual "remembers" the Forms from pre-existence, rather than extrapolating them from experience. In a 1980 *Exegesis* entry Dick affirms that "these higher realms [Plato's forms] are available, via anamnesis, during this lifetime, as Plotinus taught. . . Our spatiotemporal realm is in a certain sense, the sense that Plato taught, only semireal. What is real is. . . the morphologically-arranged upper realm, which is not separated from this realm by time or space but hier-archically."[27] The Absolute breaks into our world through either anamnesis or revelation, which Dick seems to have considered identical experiences. It is by these methods that we perceive ultimate reality.

What is the nature of the authentic reality that revelation makes apparent? How does Dick describe the encounter with God? In a 1981 interview, he gives a distinctly Christian account of this experience:

> In fact I did see the Apocalypse. I saw it. The world transformed into the apocalypse. I didn't know it at the time, but now I've read the Bible. I saw what appears in the two apocalyptic books of the Bible, Daniel and Revelation. I actually saw the apocalyptic reality underlying our reality. I didn't even know what I was seeing, except it had something to do with the Bible. Later on I was reading and discovered that this is what Daniel's vision had been. Which is deliberately reiterated by John of Patmos in Revelations. . . I saw the world (in Latin:) "under the aspect of eternity." It was under the aspect of the Apocalypse, because this was an apocalyptic vision of the world. . . It wasn't like an alternate reality, it was like what I call "trans-temporal constancy." It was like this covering has been removed, the veils which were covering it, and I was seeing something which was true now and had been true for 2,000 years. Or more than 2,000 years. Back to the time of Daniel, back to the time of the Old Testament. It was

---

[26] Dick, *Selected Letters: 1974*, 145.
[27] Dick, *In Pursuit of Valis*, 101-2.

literally outside of time and space. It was always true. It was an eternal truth, like Plato's archetypal world, where everything was always here and always now. And had been that way and would be that way.[28]

Absolute reality is eternity, that which does not change, and John's Apocalypse and the visions of Daniel describe the return of the world to this reality. The eschaton is the ultimate equation of God's reality with the reality experienced by mankind; and since God's reality is all that truly exists, any individual revelation may seem apocalyptic. The true core of this apocalyptic vision lies in Dick's reference to the world of Platonic forms, in which "everything was always here and always now," which is to say an omnipresent (and omnitemporal) state of existence. If God does exist and is the only authentic reality, then God's transcendent omnipresence is a sometimes-perceivable truth underlying our existence. Thus, Christ's return to this world—the Parousia—has already happened, we need only alter our perception so that we can comprehend it. Dick expands on this idea in a 1975 *Exegesis* entry, claiming the Parousia has arrived not "in any universal or objective sense, but surely *for me*, as an individual. . . If as Meister Eckhart says, the Kingdom of God is within the Soul of each person. . . then is not the entire realm of *Parousia*, all of it, within the inner individual soul of one person-at-a-time?"[29] Revelation, for Dick as for countless other religious thinkers before him, is "death before dying," experiencing eschatological events without oneself or the world being destroyed. The phenomenal world is *subjectively* destroyed for the one who experiences this, and in its place is left only the divine reality. The end of the world is merely the final identification of authentic reality with perceived reality, and Dick identifies revelation as the experience of this without the objective end of the phenomenal world. It is this world of eternity that alone has true existence beneath reality's veil.

GOD IN THE GUTTER: THE THEOLOGY OF OBSCURITY

The fact that we can only experience God through revelation shows that He is normally hidden within our domain, the created universe. But why must God be concealed in our world, rather than apparent? Dick asks this question

---

[28] Rickman, *Last Testament*, 34-36.
[29] Dick, *In Pursuit of Valis*, 26.

in a 1977 speech: "It is said that Christianity, Judaism, and Islam are revealed religions. Our God is the *deus absconditus*: the hidden god. But why? Why is it necessary that we be deceived regarding the nature of our reality? Why has he cloaked himself as a plurality of unrelated objects and his movements as a plurality of chance processes?"[30] The answers to these questions may well be unknowable, but Dick usually returns to the idea that the universe is undergoing a process of purification. In order for this purification to occur, God must hide himself in the phenomenal world. He must not be detected by the evil of which he is purifying creation, and so he manifests himself in the world where he is least likely to be found. As narrator-Phil states in *VALIS*, "the symbols of the divine show up in our world initially at the trash stratum... The divine intrudes where you least expect it."[31] This is the explanation for Christ's incarnation in the person of Jesus, a poor carpenter rather than the powerful political leader that first-century Jews expected the Messiah to be. Because our world is hostile to the divine, it conceals itself by displaying properties opposite to its actual nature: where God is glorious, His manifestation appears contemptible; where he is powerful, he appears powerless. This is a further implication of Paul's statement that we see "as through a glass, darkly." Dick further explains in a poetic 1975 *Exegesis* entry:

> The architect of our world, to help us, came here as our servant, disguised, to toil for us. We have seen him many times but not recognized him; maybe he is ugly in appearance, but with a good heart. Perhaps sometimes when he comes here he has forgotten his own origin, his godly power; he toils for us unaware of his true nature and what he could do to us if he remembered. For one thing, if we realized that this crippled misshapen thing was our creator, we would be disappointed. Would reject and despise him. Out of courtesy to us he hides his identity from us while here.
> One can see from this that that which we kick off to one side of the road, out of the way, which feels the toe of our boot—that may well be our God, albeit unprotesting, only showing pain in his eyes, that old, old pain which he knows so well. I notice, though, that although we kick him off to one side in pain, we do let him toil for us; we accept that. We accept his work, his offerings, his help; but him we kick away. He could reveal himself, but he would then spoil our illusion of a beautiful god. But he doesn't look evil like

---

[30] Dick, "If You Find This World Bad, You Should See Some of the Others." In Sutin, ed., *Shifting Realities*, 253.
[31] Dick, *VALIS*, 228 (§14).

Satan; just homely. Unworthy. Also, although he has vast creative and building power, and judgment, he is not clever. He is not a bright god. Often he is too dumb to know when he's being teased or insulted; it takes physical pain, rather than mere scorn, to register.

Ugly like this, despised and teased and tormented and finally put to death, he returned shining and transfigured; our Savior, Jesus Christ (before him Ikhnaton, Zoroaster, etc; Hefestus). When He returned we saw Him as he really is—that is, not by surface appearance. His radiance, his essence, like Light. The God of Light wears a humble and plain shell here. (Like a metamorphosis of some humble toiling beetle).[32]

For Dick, Christ will not return riding a white horse, but rather in the form of a beetle, a beggar, or an empty beer can kicked to the side of the road. God, though remaining all-powerful, allows himself to be made weak and to appear defeated in this world. But his moment of apparent defeat is truly his moment of final victory: Christ's death on the cross is the moment that assures the salvation of humankind.

In this concept of the *deus absconditus* Dick's theology overlaps with that of Martin Luther.[33] Luther's "theology of the cross" depends on just such a view of God's hiddenness in wretched and helpless forms in our world. Luther articulates this view in his *Heidelberg Disputation*:

> The manifest and visible things of God are placed in opposition to the invisible, namely, his human nature, weakness, fool-ishness ... Because men misused the knowledge of God through works, God wished again to be recognized in suffering, and to condemn wisdom concerning invisible things by means of wisdom concerning visible things, so that those who did not honor God as manifested in his works should honor him as he is hidden in his suffering... It is not sufficient for anyone, and it does him no good to recognize God in his glory and majesty, unless he recognizes him in the humility and shame of the cross. Thus God destroys the wisdom of the wise, as Isa. [45:15] says, "Truly, thou art a God who hidest himself."[34]

---

[32] Dick, *Selected Letters: 1975-1976*, 32-33.

[33] Dick certainly read Luther, as he cites him on several occasions. In the *Exegesis* excerpts published thus far, he does not refer specifically to Luther's "theology of the cross," but even if there is no direct influence, there is a striking similarity between the beliefs of the two writers. My comparison here is not to suggest such an influence, but rather to use Luther's thought to illuminate Dick's ideas.

[34] Martin Luther, "Heidelberg Disputation." Trans. Harold J. Grimm. In *Luther's Works*, vol. 31, ed. Harold J. Grimm and Helmut T. Lehmann. Philadelphia: Muhlenberg Press, 1957, 52-53.

Luther, like Dick, sees God not in his glory, but rather concealed within the cross, manifested as the opposite of an omnipotent being. Regarding this "theology of the cross," Alister McGrath states that "*Deus absconditus* is the God who is hidden *in* his revelation. The revelation of God in the cross lies *abscondita sub contrario*, so that God's strength is revealed under apparent weakness, and his wisdom under apparent folly... Only faith perceives the real situation which underlies the apparent situation."[35] The fact that God reveals himself requires him to be hidden; but he is hidden even within that revelation. Jews at the time of Jesus did not expect the Messiah to be put to death, let alone in so disgraceful a manner as crucifixion. God, then, is *not* apparent in his primary revelation, that is, in the person of Jesus. Rather, in this most important manifestation, God requires faith in opposition to reason and the senses in order to be truly honored. Luther saw God's hiddenness on the cross as necessary to his true revelation.

Luther focused on God's hiddenness within the cross and the incarnation of Christ. Dick expanded the idea of the *deus absconditus* to include "the trash in the gutter." In a 1978 *Exegesis* entry, Dick further illustrates this idea: "the true God mimics the universe, the very region he has invaded; he takes on the likeness of sticks & trees & cans in gutters—he presumes to be trash discarded, debris no longer noticed. Lurking, the true God literally ambushes reality and us as well."[36] Dick's God slowly infiltrates our world at its lowest level; in rubbish, pop songs, and pulp novels, he reaches out to save individuals without being detected by the forces that wish to destroy him. Dick saw confirmation of this theory with the release of the film *Star Wars* in 1977, as he explains in a letter from that year: "God speaks to us from popular novels and films; here is a supreme example. Names and creeds and doctrines and dogmas and formulations are not important; what is important is the living Word. And it is that which Lucas depicts and describes in 'the force,' as he calls it. And people everywhere are responding."[37] Dick saw the hiddenness of God's message in popular forms as a modern version of Christ's hiddenness. Christ, incarnated as Jesus, hid his saving *logos* from the authorities both by incarnating himself at the lowest level of society and by hiding his message in the form of parables. Dick speculates in a 1975

---

[35] Alister McGrath, *Luther's Theology of the Cross*. Oxford: Basil Blackwell Inc., 1985, 165.
[36] Dick, *In Pursuit of Valis*, 223.
[37] Dick, *Selected Letters: 1977-1979*, 103.

Exegesis entry on the secret meanings of Christ's teachings: "*Mark* 4:11 says that the parables were intended to confuse and not inform everyone except the disciples, the latter understanding the esoteric meaning, the outsiders getting only the exoteric meaning which would fail to save them; this was especially true regarding parables about the approaching Kingdom of God... The written gospels record probably mostly the exoteric parable meanings, not the inner core."[38] Jesus, in addition to hiding his true nature by appearing—even if it was only appearance—as a powerless person, rather than an infinitely powerful manifestation of God, hid his true message within parables. In the same entry, Dick further speculates that there may be a new manifestation of God that will eventually encompass not only the elect who choose to understand God's message, but rather all creation. This New Covenant must begin somewhere, however, and Dick came to believe that it would begin, as it did in Jesus' lifetime, at the lowest levels of society. Dick states that God "is found at the outskirts or trash or bottom level of this world, as far from the imperial *omphalos* of power as possible. This would adequately account for the way Jesus appeared at the First Advent. But the Second Advent... will consist of a direct & successful attack on the inner fortress of imperial power itself."[39] The teleology of God in the universe points to a time when God is no longer hidden, but rather makes his omnipotence wholly apparent in all levels of existence.

In what way will God re-enter the universe? Dick described God's perpetual "ambush" of the world in terms of transubstantiation, as in this 1979 *Exegesis* entry: "God can transubstantiate the epiphenomenon into the real, by virtue of his immanent presence in it, as in the eucharist. Thus reality is viewed as a perpetual sacrament: with the formal eucharist as a micro-enactment of a continual macrocosmic ongoing process which I actually *saw*. The real, then, is sacred, even at the trash stratum, due to this transubstantiation."[40] God, or part of God, is gradually replacing the substance of our unreal world with his own substance, mimicking objects made no longer from debased material but rather from God's incorruptible body. In his explorations of this subject, Dick often referred to God as "Zebra," a reference to the camouflage offered by an individual zebra's

---

[38] Dick, *In Pursuit of Valis*, 31.
[39] Dick, *In Pursuit of Valis*, 73.
[40] Dick, *In Pursuit of Valis*, 44.

stripes when it stands with a herd.[41] In a 1977 letter, Dick further describes the concept: "Zebra mimics our reality. In a sense Zebra *is* our reality, posing as an infinitude of separate objects (called by the Greek philosophers 'the many'). In actuality, all these many separate objects—and their transformations and processes—are 'the One,' which is to say, Zebra."[42] Zebra, the mimicking being, does not simply *pretend* to be our reality, as this comparison to Brahman shows. In some sense its mimicry is more authentic than the objects themselves which it mimics; its divine fakery is more real than our mundane actuality.

An outline for one of the many early drafts of *VALIS*, written in a 1977 letter, contains an early, fictionalized concept of the Zebra concept. In the outline, a government agent named Houston Paige has learned of the existence of a mimicking life form that he, and the corrupt government, believes to be an enemy of the state. Paige attempts to detect this mimicking being, but cannot because he does not realize how vast it is:

> Zebra is enormous in physical size. . . [and] in fact spans thousands, possibly even millions of miles of our space. . . Paige can't detect Zebra because he is inside Zebra every day of his life. In fact a portion of Zebra has assimilated the police computers which predicted the theoretical existence of Zebra. When Paige drinks an Old Fashioned, Zebra is the bottle of bourbon, the ice, the slice of orange, the bitters, the glass. When Paige takes notes on the probable characteristics of Zebra, Zebra is the ballpoint pen, clipboard, and paper.[43]

The Zebra concept is thus a science-fictionalized allegory of the idea that God is hidden in our world, with a mimicking alien being substituted for God. Dick related the Zebra idea to the Hindu concept of Brahman in a 1977 letter, explaining the origin of the idea in the science-fictional question, "What if Brahman is a computer?"[44] But in the same letter he also notes its resemblance to Pierre Teilhard de Chardin's idea of the cosmic or Universal Christ. Teilhard de Chardin describes God's action in the world as "God gathering to himself not merely a diffuse multiplicity of souls, but the solid, organic, reality of a universe, taken from top to bottom

---

[41] Lawrence Sutin, "Selected Significant Terms." In Dick, *In Pursuit of Valis*, 271.
[42] Dick, *Selected Letters: 1977-1979*, 67.
[43] Dick, *Selected Letters: 1977-1979*, 12.
[44] Dick, *Selected Letters: 1977-1979*, 67.

in the complete extent and unity of its energies."[45] Teilhard de Chardin further describes this as a substantial transformation of the universe into God: "In order to create... God has inevitably to immerse himself in the multiple, so that he may incorporate it into himself."[46] Dick is in complete agreement with Teilhard de Chardin here, and in the *Exegesis* he frequently acknowledged the similarities between their theories. In Dick's terms, this incorporation is a form of transubstantiation: God, as a mimicking, undetectable being superior to human beings, is altering the substance of the universe and infusing it with and thus incorporating it into his infinite Being.

The concept of transubstantiation was not new to Dick; he had become fascinated with it soon after his 1963 conversion to the Episcopalian Church, and his research in the subject formed much of the basis for the metaphysics of *The Three Stigmata of Palmer Eldritch*.[47] Dick acknowledges this connection in a 1977 *Exegesis* entry:

> When I recently reread STIGMATA I saw it for what it was: a penetrating, acute and exhaustive study of the miracle of transubstantiation, simply reversing the bipolarities of good & evil. What the novel contemplated was—that is, the conclusion it reached—was the startling notion that imbibing of the sacred host culminated, for the imbiber, in eventually becoming the deity of which the host was the supernatural manifestation of [sic]. Since all of them were consuming hosts of the same deity, they all became the same deity, and their separate or human identities were abolished. They literally became the deity, all of them, one after another. What this constituted in the novel was an eerie kind of invasion. They were invaded on an individual basis and they were, regarded in another way, invaded as a planet or species, etc., which is to say collectively.[48]

Eldritch is an evil deity, and so this invasion is a diabolical one. But since Zebra is a benevolent God, his invasion is a salvific enterprise by which the universe is ultimately and irreversibly transformed into the mystical body of Christ.

---

[45] Pierre Teilhard de Chardin, "The Awaited Word." In *Toward the Future*. Trans. René Hague. New York: Harcourt Brace Jovanovich, 1975, 97.

[46] Teilhard de Chardin, "My Fundamental Vision." In *Toward the Future*, 196.

[47] Rickman, *Last Testament*, 10. The Eucharist was also an important theme in both *The Divine Invasion* and *The Transmigration of Timothy Archer*; see Chapter 1 above.

[48] Dick, *In Pursuit of Valis*, 171. See also Dick, *Selected Letters: 1977-1979*, 134-135.

In this case, too, Dick's thought is similar (though by no means identical) to that of Martin Luther.[49] Luther argued against both the Catholic Church and the most radical Protestants regarding the Eucharist and the question of transubstantiation. The former, drawing from Aristotelian philosophy, held that God's substance replaced that of the bread and wine during the Mass, and hence became wholly God. The latter argued that the bread and wine remained simply bread and wine, and that God's substance could not enter them. Luther argued for a middle road between these two views, holding that the body of Christ existed everywhere, within all things, and thus was unquestionably present in the Eucharistic meal without replacing either of them. Of Christ's omnipresence Luther writes: "He is above all creatures and in and beyond all creatures. . . Therefore he now has all things before his eyes, more than I have you before my eyes, and he is closer to us than any creature is to another."[50] Though Christ's body is present everywhere, it can only be found where he wishes us to find it, as Luther further explains: "Although he is present in all creatures, and I might find him in stone, in fire, in water, or even in a rope, for he certainly is there, yet he does not wish that I seek him there apart from the Word. . . He is present everywhere, but he does not wish that you grope for him everywhere. Grope rather where the Word is, and there you will lay hold of him in the right way."[51] God *can* be found anywhere, but if we search for him everywhere, we become scattered, and are likely to become devoted to things in which God is rather than to God himself. The Eucharist thus focuses our search for God. When we search for Christ in the Eucharist and partake of the bread and wine, we become a purified part of God: "So it is true that we Christians are the spiritual body of Christ and collectively one loaf, one drink, one spirit. All this is achieved by Christ, who through his own body makes us all to be one spiritual body; so that all of us partake equally of his body, and are therefore equal and united with one another. Likewise, the fact that we consume one bread and

---

[49] Dick may well have read Luther's writings on the Eucharist in his research on the subject, but he does not cite him specifically on the matter. Nonetheless, Luther's writings illuminate the subject quite well, and are helpful to understanding Dick's ideas about transubstantiation even if there was no direct influence.
[50] Martin Luther, "The Sacrament of the Body and Blood of Christ—Against the Fanatics." Trans. Frederick C. Ahrens. In *Luther's Works*, vol. 36, ed. Abdel Ross Wentz and Helmut T. Lehmann. Philadelphia: Muhlenberg Press, 1957, 342.
[51] Luther, "The Sacrament—Against the Fanatics." In *Luther's Works*, vol. 36, 342.

drink makes us to be one bread and drink."[52] The host that we consume is transcendently a part of God's body, and consuming God's body causes one to become a part of God, just as Dick describes in *The Three Stigmata*.

Dick does not feel, however, that God is only accessible to us in the bread and wine of the Eucharist. Rather, he believes that the process of Zebra's mimicry of the world creates an ever-increasing number of places and things through which God may be reached. It is unclear whether Dick believes, as did Luther, that Christ's body already permeates the entire phenomenal world. At times he states that the mimicry process is slow and gradual; that only select parts of the phenomenal world have been made real. But elsewhere he declares that the process is complete, as in this 1978 *Exegesis* entry: "Authentic reality has breached through into our world—which signifies that the end times have come (maybe long ago) but the irreal, the hologram, effaces it from our perception... Zebra... *has come already*."[53] It is possible that the world has already been "transubstantiated" into the real—that is, into God's being—and that only an illusory hologram remains. The Apocalypse is merely the destruction of this hologram and the revelation of the authentic, divine nature of reality.

For Dick the Eucharist is a reflection and a reminder of Christ's death and resurrection. But it is also a symbol of God's continual reentry into the universe, his process of invasion. The concept of bread and wine becoming or sharing in Christ's body reflects the manner in which God is currently transforming our world.[54] Dick believed the Eucharist to be an act that occurs in eternity, outside of linear time, as he writes in a 1976 letter: "When we celebrate the Last Supper, it is a true statement to say that it is the actual event itself, not a mere reenactment or ritual remembrance; Christ, having

---

[52] Martin Luther, "The Adoration of the Sacrament." Trans. Abdel Ross Wentz. In *Luther's Works*, vol. 36, ed. Abdel Ross Wentz and Helmut T. Lehmann. Philadelphia: Muhlenberg Press, 1957, 286.

[53] Dick, *In Pursuit of Valis*, 74, emphasis in original.

[54] Dick does not seem to have taken a side regarding the debate in the Reformation over transubstantiation. Though he clearly does not believe, as did more radical protestants, that the bread and wine are simply that, he makes no definitive statements whether the substance of the meal is completely replaced by the substance of God (as per Catholic doctrine) or if God exists "with, in, and under" the bread and wine (as Luther argued). His use of the word "transubstantiation" is not a statement of belief on this matter, but rather a more general reference to God's action in the Sacrament of the Eucharist.

been there at the Last Supper, is here now each time it is enacted. This is not metaphor. It is not poetry. It is real."[55] Christ, as an eternal being, penetrates the veil of time whenever the Eucharist is enacted, becoming actually present. Similarly, Christ's Passion, which is reflected in the Eucharist, is an eternal act. It is the work of salvation that occurs outside of linear time, as Dick describes in a 1979 *Exegesis* entry: "The stages of the sequence are enacted by Jesus in his passion, his death and resurrection, the Cross itself. The sequence, then, must finally be understood as the Way of the Cross, which is not physical but is, rather, the journey of the soul, perpetually re-enacted. The Gospels, then, depict a sacred mythic rite outside of time, rather than an historical event."[56] Christ's Passion—his redemptive death and resurrection—was not something that occurred in the past, but something that is occurring now and that occurs perpetually in eternity. In our world, it is revealed in God's action of mimicry, hiding himself in the "trash layers" of our world by infusing the everyday with his eternal substance. Christ's suffering, God's hiddenness in the cross, and the secrecy of Jesus' teaching are reflected in *all* suffering in our world, in *all* secret divine messages, be they in parables, pulp novels, or rubbish in an alley.

This is the essence of Dick's theology of obscurity: that "*By the very nature* [sic] *it is deus absconditus, but hidden close by ("Break a stick & there is Jesus")*. One can reread and reinterpret all scripture from the vantage point of this understanding."[57] God's messages *must* be hidden, because our world is backwards, a mirror image of authentic reality. The glorious must appear humble, the strong weak, the wise foolish. It is for this reason, Dick came to believe, that he had been chosen (in the times when he believed he *had* been chosen) to receive his revelation: that he was able to conceal God's message to him in the "trashy" genre of SF. In a 1982 interview Dick declared that "I belong to the trash stratum and my work is a genre work, I write science fiction. Many people regard it as trash."[58] Dick himself acknowledged the "trashy" nature of his writing, or at least of the genre in which he worked. But he did not feel this degraded his writing—rather, because God chooses to enter the phenomenal world at the level of trash, he seems to have felt his work was elevated by being debased. This seems to have been one of Dick's

---

[55] Dick, *Selected Letters: 1975-1976*, 64.
[56] Dick, *In Pursuit of Valis*, 95.
[57] Dick, *In Pursuit of Valis*, 76, emphasis in original.
[58] Rickman, *Last Testament*, 142.

rationales for opposing attempts to make SF "acceptable" for scholarly study—by making it seem respectable, it is brought out of the gutter and hence away from the preferred area of the divine.

Why must God confine himself to the lowest levels of this world? What is the purpose of a salvific power that conceals itself? In the same 1982 interview, Dick explains God's rationale for hiding at the level of trash:

> He picked real stupid dopey people. I mean it's part of his strategy. That way you have, the recipient has the option to discard the whole thing. It forces the recipient to do what nobody will do and that is read the messages themselves and draw their own conclusion. What they do is they pick up the book, look at the cover, turn it over, hold it open like this and throw it down and they don't know what, if I ask them "What did it say?" They won't know. They see but they do not see. They look but they do not look. They hear but they do not hear. But someday they will remember it was handed to them.[59]

The salvific message is there for us to see, and by hiding his message in "trash," God can guarantee that everyone will see it and be given the chance to believe. By hiding himself, God grants to those who view his messages the ability to choose for themselves whether or not to believe them. If God were apparent, there would be no questioning his authority and power; all would be obligated to acknowledge him without consideration or choice. Since he is hidden, however, those who follow God must do so of their own will, after evaluating his hidden messages and developing faith. Dick also theorized that God must hide so that evil separates itself from good, as described in a 1977 letter: "If God remains continually concealed from us all, the fallen angels among us will make the error of believing that they are unobserved, and will act out existentially their evil nature, their ontological evil, and so be visible in contrast to the rest of us."[60] If God were apparent, evil would hide itself, becoming virtually indistinguishable from good. Thus God's hiding from us is actually a means of helping us, making it easier for us to detect the evil that wishes harm the good. In the terms of an *Exegesis* entry quoted above, God is that which we kick into the gutter, but which also "toils for us" without our knowledge. Our conception of God's glory, if not tempered with faith, would be ruined by the reality of a humble, ugly, toiling god. The eyes of faith are able to see glory *within* the hidden, toiling action

---

[59] Rickman, *Last Testament*, 176.
[60] Dick, *Selected Letters: 1977-1979*, 92.

of God, whereas those who would expect to see only God's glorious side would leave out the work by which salvation is wrought. Again, this view is similar to Martin Luther's, of whose ideas McGrath writes: "Far from regarding suffering or evil as a nonsensical intrusion into the world (which Luther regards as the opinion of a 'theologian of glory'), the 'theologian of the cross' regards such suffering as his most precious treasure, for revealed and yet hidden in precisely such sufferings is none other than the living God, working out the salvation of those whom he loves."[61] Dick, of course, sees God not only hidden in the cross, but in nearly every debased part of the world as well, and through the action of "Zebra," those parts of the world in which God is hidden and revealed is ever-growing.

Dick's theology, which might be termed the "theology of obscurity," may seem, at first glance, quite pessimistic. Rather than seeing God positively reflected in all things, it offers us the concept of a God to whom creation is hostile; who must hide himself within his own universe at the risk of being driven out or killed. Further, God's hiddenness makes him seem nearly impossible to uncover. But Dick's message is rather an inclusive one that makes the divine accessible to everyone. Just as, in the words of Paul, "Christ Jesus came into the world to save sinners" (1 Ti 1:15), Dick's message is that God in the present day speaks to the poor, the weary, and the science-fiction fans. A 1978 *Exegesis* entry explores this:

> "Where should you most expect to find God?" A.: "In the least likely place." I discern from this the following: "In point of fact you therefore cannot find God at all; he must—will—find you, & *when* & where you least expect it"—i.e., he will take you by surprise, like the still small voice which Elijah heard. . . So my writing—itself part of the "gutter" & as [SF writer Stanislaw] Lem says, "Piling trash upon trash"—may serve as the sort of gadfly thing that Socrates considered himself to act as. My writing is a *very* unlikely place to expect to encounter the Holy.[62]

God hides, but Dick was certain that he *will* find us all in time. That he is hidden at the "trash stratum" simply means that he will find those who need most to be found first; that it is at the lowest levels of existence that the most work can be done. God's self-hiddenness is a message of friendship to common people, an assurance that that which is apparently worthless in this

---

[61] McGrath, *Luther's Theology of the Cross*, 151.
[62] Dick, *In Pursuit of Valis*, 156-7.

world is—and will be—most valuable in eternity.

Radio Free Albemuth contains a passage that beautifully conveys the optimism of the concept of God's obscurity:

> I spent one whole day walking around Placentia [California], enjoying myself immensely. There was a beauty in the trash of the alleys which I had never noticed before; my vision now seemed sharpened, rather than impaired. As I walked along it seemed to me that the flattened beer cans and papers and weeds and junk mail had been arranged by the wind into patterns; these patterns, when I scrutinized them, lay distributed so as to comprise a visual language. It resembled the trail signs which I understood American Indians used, and as I walked along I felt the invisible presence of a great spirit which had gone before me—walked here and moved the unwanted debris in these subtle, meaningful ways so as to spell out a greeting of comradeship to me, the smaller one who would follow.[63]

God's obscurity lets us know that all debris—be it physical trash or the "debris" of humanity—is absolutely essential to the plan, the *logos*, of all Creation. In this, the theology of obscurity is ultimately, transcendentally optimistic.

WORDS AND THINGS:
DICK'S IMPORTANCE AS A MODERN THEOLOGIAN

What does Philip K. Dick's experience, and his extensive writing about that experience, add to modern theology? What makes Dick important as a religious thinker? To begin, we must examine how Dick's encounters function as both experience and "scripture" to be examined, and how the *Exegesis*—the examination of experience—functions as both scripture and further experience. Dick's writing can be considered as a valuable contribution to the debate over the nature of "mystical experience" and the relation of experience to interpretation. Scholar Steven Katz, arguing from the basis "that there are *no* pure (i.e. unmediated) experiences," claims that there is no meaningful division between an experience and the report of it: "Whatever the truth of the nature of the commingling of theory, experience and interpretation that goes into the mystics' 'report', the *only* evidence one

---

[63] Dick, *Radio Free Albemuth*, 126-127 (§18).

has to call upon to support one's analysis of this material, and hence one's description of this relationship, is the given recording of the mystic—the already 'experienced' and 'interpreted' first person recording."[64] Katz calls into question the idea that an experience can somehow be segregated either from an account of it or prior accounts with which the mystic was familiar, since, according to Katz, mystics base their experiences on the experiences of mystics who have gone before them. Their reports are not interpretations of the "ineffable," but rather are a product of and a reinforcement of the culture from which they develop. Ninian Smart, in a similar vein, argues that "the distinction between experience and interpretation is not clear cut . . . [because] the concepts used in describing and explaining an experience vary in their degree of ramification. That is to say, where a concept occurs as part of a doctrinal scheme it gains its meaning in part from a range of doctrinal statements taken to be true."[65] The report of a mystic, according to Smart, is inseparable from the culture from which it springs, and the "interpretation" and the "experience" thus commingle and cannot be isolated. Katz and Smart stand in opposition to the viewpoint of some, such as Aldous Huxley, who argue that all mystical experience is essentially the same across cultures. This view holds that all authentic mystics have encountered the Ground of existence, and the differences in their reports are only due to the mystics' interpretations for their individual cultures, not a fundamental difference in experience. Huxley, in *The Perennial Philosophy*, states that some mystics "have left accounts of the Reality they were thus enabled to apprehend and have tried to relate, in one comprehensive system of thought, the given facts of this experience with the given facts of their other experiences."[66] Similarly, Evelyn Underhill wishes to clarify "the difference between [mysticism's] substance and its accidents: between traditional forms and methods, and the eternal experience which they have mediated. In mystical literature words are frequently confused with things, and symbols with realities; so that

---

[64] Steven Katz, "The 'Conservative' Character of Mystical Experience." In Katz, ed., *Mysticism and Religious Traditions*. New York: Oxford University Press, 1983, 3 and 5. Emphasis in original.

[65] Ninian Smart, "Interpretation and Mystical Experience." In Richard Woods, ed., *Understanding Mysticism*. New York: Doubleday, 1980, 82.

[66] Aldous Huxley, *The Perennial Philosophy*. 1944; rpt. New York: Harper and Row, 1970, ix.

much of this literature seems to the reader to refer to some self-consistent and exclusive dreamworld, and not to the achievement of universal truth."[67] Language, to those who hold this viewpoint, is a barrier, and hence reports of mysticism are in some ways frustrating: the mystic has had a revelation of truth, but the articulation of that truth cannot completely convey it, at best it can only point the way to a similar experience. Huxley explains this problem of language: "The subject matter of the Perennial Philosophy is the nature of eternal, spiritual Reality; but the language in which it must be formulated was developed for the purpose of dealing with phenomena in time. . . . The nature of Truth-the-Fact cannot be described by means of verbal symbols that do not adequately correspond to it."[68] The "perennialist" viewpoint holds that mystical experience is beyond language, and thus even the most inspired writing cannot adequately convey it. Scholars such as Katz hold a quite different opinion: that language *creates* the experience. Rather than an attempt to describe the indescribable, a mystic's report is, for Katz, an extension of the culture of which the mystic is part. There is no experience followed by interpretation; interpretation precedes, follows, and co-exists with the experience, and the two cannot be isolated.

Dick adds a new perspective to the debate over the nature of mysticism. He did not believe that his experience was simply a creation of language or culture; rather, he believed it to be an authentic divine revelation. But this does not mean, as Huxley and Underhill suggest, that he had somehow grasped truths that he could not communicate. Dick believed that his experience was unmediated, but it was also unclear. Thus he wrote the 8,000 page *Exegesis* with the hope of uncovering the Truth that he was convinced was hidden somewhere in his experience. For Dick, writing about religious experience is a form of religious experience in itself. The testing of new theories, as displayed in the endless pages of the *Exegesis*, are not merely a collection of reports about a religious experience, but rather formed a sort of expansion of the initial experience. Paul Williams explains: "He lived for the pursuit of truth, and the world in which that pursuit took place was for him the world of pen . . . and paper. . . It is not that he pursued the thought and then wrote down his conclusions. He pursued *by* writing—that is the realm where the action took place, that is where he lived so much of

---

[67] Evelyn Underhill, "The Essentials of Mysticism." In Richard Woods, ed., *Understanding Mysticism.* New York: Doubleday, 1980, 26.
[68] Huxley, *The Perennial Philosophy,* 128.

his life. . . [Dick's writing is] not a record of his experiences, . . . but the experience itself."[69] The countless epiphanies of the *Exegesis* are recorded not *after* they happened, but rather were brought out *during* the act of writing. Words, for Dick, are not a barrier as for Huxley and Underhill, but rather a doorway through which Truth can sometimes be glimpsed. Dick's writing offers the view that intellectual analysis is both a form and a cause of religious experience, and further, if that analysis is done in the act of writing, the writing is inseparable from the experience it causes. Lawrence Sutin states that "Dick genuinely believed that, by sufficient pondering and analysis, the truth of 2-3-74, and of reality itself, might just be revealed to him. Despite the vivid experiential nature of 2-3-74, Dick kept faith in intellectual analysis—and not in further experience *a la* meditation or an attempted recreation of the factors that led to 2-3-74 as the key to truth."[70] Given a mystical experience that was confusing rather than illuminating, that gave more questions than answers, Dick was unable to give a report of his experience that could convey a mystical "truth." Rather, he endlessly analyzed his noetic experience, always hoping to uncover the truth he believed lurked within it.

Dick, if his experience can be called "mysticism" at all, presents us with *two types* of mystical experience: 1) an initial, possibly ineffable, experience, and 2) an intellectual experience arising from attempts after the fact at interpreting the primary experience. The interpretation of the initial experience cannot be segregated from it, but rather is presupposed by the unclear and open-ended nature of that experience. Dick, since his experience did not present him with clear answers, could not help but wonder about the meaning of 2-3-74. The intellectual process of theorizing *directly proceeds* from the inexplicable experience, and since it is a search for an illuminating truth, filled (as Dick's style in the *Exegesis* shows) with periodic, if short-lived, epiphanies, this intellectual search is an experience in itself. As the report of the 11-17-80 theophany shows, the intellectual process leads to infinity—to God—and Dick believed that this game may have been the ultimate purpose of his initial experiences. Dick's religious writings contribute to the debate over mystical experience, as well as offering insight into their author's unique life.

[69] Williams, *Only Apparently Real*, 24.
[70] Lawrence Sutin, "Preface: On the Exegesis of Philip K. Dick." In Dick, *In Pursuit of Valis*, xii.

Dick's eight-year quest for the meaning of his religious experience, as well as the longer philosophical quest begun in his earliest writing, offers no definite ontological answers. But this lack of a conclusive culmination does not prevent Dick from being an original and lively theologian. The value of Dick's thought is not in the structures of the belief systems that he laid out, but rather in their variety. Like his fiction, his theology is speculative. In his SF, he created new worlds in space and time, and in his religious writing he created new worlds of the spirit, both human and divine. But not only Dick's answers are valuable and original: Dick is important as a modern theologian due to the questions he asks and the manner of their formulation. The division of his inquiry into the two questions of humanity and reality—perhaps the basic categories of any ontological inquiry—focused his lifelong philosophical quest, allowing the *Exegesis* to be an insightful and exciting intellectual exercise. It is a complex and sometimes convoluted text, but it is an invaluable document of one man's search for meaning. Even if a definite meaning eluded him, Dick's search itself is still full of an exciting vitality, and his religious thought is certain to become an invaluable part of the future world of the spirit.

APPENDIX:

Biographical Notes on Philip K. Dick*

Philip Kindred Dick and his twin sister, Jane Charlotte, were born on December 16, 1928, to Dorothy and Edgar Dick in Chicago. The twins were born premature, and this, combined with their parents' poverty, a particularly harsh winter, and an injury Jane received when only a few weeks old, led to Jane's death a little over a month later. His sister's death was a uniquely intense trauma for Philip, and Sutin claims that it was "the central event of Phil's psychic life. The torment extended throughout his life, manifesting itself in difficult relations with women and fascination with resolving dualist (twin-poled) dilemmas."[1] Several of Dick's novels include "twin" characters: perhaps most notable is the 1965 novel *Dr. Bloodmoney*, in which a young girl is found to have a vestigial twin insider her body who is able to communicate telepathically with both his host/sister and the souls of the dead. Though Dick's sister was only with him for a month, she nonetheless became infinitely important to him. In addition to this trauma, Dick's parents divorced in 1933, and he remained with his mother, with whom he was to have a less-than-happy relationship. Psychologically, Dick was a troubled child; he saw several psychiatrists in elementary school and junior high as he developed agoraphobia and various anxiety disorders.

Despite this, Dick was a precocious child, and became fascinated with writing at a very young age. He wrote his first novel, a Swift-inspired work called *Return to Lilliput*, at the age of fourteen. The manuscript, sadly, is not extant. It is likely that Dick wrote other long works throughout his adolescence, though, like this first work, the manuscripts no longer exist. After high school, Dick began work in a record store, an occupation that enhanced his love of music and inspired him deeply: even in his final novels over 30 years later, many of Dick's characters work in some part of the music industry. Dick married for the first time in 1948 to Jeanette Morlin; the

---

* This appendix draws primarily on Lawrence Sutin's biography, *Divine Invasions: A Life of Philip K. Dick* (New York: Citadel Press/Carol Publishing Group, 1991).
[1] Sutin, *Divine Invasions*, 12.

marriage lasted only six months. After their divorce, Dick enrolled briefly at the University of California at Berkeley to study philosophy. This, too, lasted only a few months.

Dick married again in 1949 to Kleo Apostolides, with whom he stayed for eight years. In this period, Dick, who had been focusing on writing mainstream novels that never saw print in his lifetime, began writing SF under the guidance of Anthony Boucher. Boucher, editor of *The Magazine of Fantasy and Science Fiction*, bought Dick's first story, "Roog," in 1951. Realizing that, in the SF field, he could actually write for a living, Dick quickly left his job and began writing full-time at breakneck speed. By 1954, Dick was a regular in SF pulps and had published over sixty stories.

Dick soon shifted his focus to writing novels, primarily because he could make more money from novels than short stories. His first novel, *Solar Lottery*, was published in 1955; he sold two more that year. He longed to use these early SF publications as a bridge by which to publish his mainstream fiction, however. In 1956 and 1957, Dick wrote no SF at all, instead focusing on his mainstream novels; between 1952 and 1960 he wrote eleven mainstream works, only one of which saw print in his lifetime (*Confessions of a Crap Artist*, published in 1975).

Dick left Kleo in 1958 for Anne Rubenstein, marrying her in April, 1959. Anne had been married before and had three children; a year after their marriage she and Dick had a daughter, Laura Archer Dick. Dick found it difficult to work in the environment of Anne's home, and this, combined with his frustration over his inability to sell his mainstream novels, led him to consider giving up writing altogether. He gave it one last try in 1961, however, and the result—*The Man in the High Castle*—won him the Hugo award for Best Science Fiction Novel of the Year and is considered by many to be his first masterpiece. The award restored Dick's faith in his writing, and he began writing again, faster than ever before. Between 1963 and 1964 alone he completed ten more novels, all SF. In order to keep up this rapid pace, Dick began taking amphetamines, as well as experimenting with some other drugs.

Though he had never been distinctly religious, Dick joined the Episcopal Church in 1963. Sutin cites two major factors in this conversion: first, the insistence his wife, Anne, and second, a bizarre vision of a demonic face in the sky: "It was immense; it filled a quarter of the sky. It had empty slots for eyes—it was metal and cruel and, worst of all, it was God."[2] This

---

[2] Quoted in Sutin, *Divine Invasions*, 127.

bizarre, stress-induced vision was a major inspiration for *The Three Stigmata of Palmer Eldritch*. In the Episcopal Church, Dick may have hoped to find a more positive image of God than his horrific hallucination offered him. Regardless of what Dick was looking for in the Episcopal Church, he found theological doctrines that fascinated him; the miracle of transubstantiation also became a central theme in *Palmer Eldritch*.

Dick divorced Anne in early 1964. Soon afterwards, he met Nancy Hackett, whom he married two years later. In 1967, they had a daughter, Isolde Freya Dick. Their marriage became strained, however, perhaps because of Dick's increasing drug use. In 1970, Nancy left him, taking Isa with her. Dick fell into a deep depression, hardly writing at all. He became more and more enmeshed in the drug culture, opening his home to the young people of his neighborhood. His home became a central location for the trade and use of drugs, and he a sort of drug guru, though he did not take as many drugs as his younger guests. This period provided the material for Dick's 1977 anti-drug novel *A Scanner Darkly*, which examines the destructive effects Dick came to notice after several months of this lifestyle.

Fueled by drugs and fear of the police, Dick's anxiety grew in this period, but his paranoia may not have been irrational: in November, 1971, Dick's home was broken into and various papers of his, including manuscripts and cancelled checks, were stolen, but his valuables left untouched. Dick was utterly perplexed by this break-in, and spent years theorizing about who was responsible: the local police? The FBI? The Black Panthers? Fearing a conspiracy against him that he was certain would lead to his death, Dick moved to Canada in early 1972, and planned to stay there. While there, he attempted suicide and entered a rehabilitation center; for a time he quit drugs entirely, using them only occasionally for the last ten years of his life. After a few months in Canada, Dick returned to California, and soon met Tessa Busby, who was 18 years old at the time. A year later, Dick and Tessa were married, and they soon had a son, Christopher Kenneth Dick. Though this marriage, too, ended in divorce in 1977, Dick's life had finally begun to settle down after the chaos of the late 60s and early 70s, and he had begun writing again. It was in this semi-normal atmosphere in which the 2-3-74 experiences, which occupied Dick's mental life until his death of a stroke in March 1982, occurred.

WORKS CITED

Anderson, Bernhard W., et. al., eds. *The New Oxford Annotated Bible with the Apocrypha*. Oxford and New York: Oxford University Press, 1994.

Apel, D. Scott. *Philip K. Dick: The Dream Connection, Second Edition*. San Jose, California: The Impermanent Press, 1999.

Augustine, St. *Confessions, Books I-XIII*, trans. F.J. Sheed. Indianapolis/ Cambridge: Hackett, 1993.

———. *The Trinity*, trans. Edmund Hill, O.P., ed. John E. Rotell, O.S.A. Brooklyn, New York: New City Press, 1991.

———. *Augustine of Hippo: Selected Writings.* Trans. and ed. Mary T. Clark. New York: Paulist Press, 1984.

Bertrand, Frank C. "Philip K. Dick on Philosophy: A Brief Interview." *Niekas* 36, 1988, 22-24. Originally published as "Philip K. Dick et la Philosophie: Une Courte Interview," trans. by Sylvie Laine. *Yellow Submarine* 41, September 1986, 30-31. Reprinted in Philip K. Dick, *The Shifting Realities of Philip K. Dick: Selected Literary and Philosophical Writings*, ed. Lawrence Sutin. New York: Vintage/ Random House, 1995, 44-47.

Blake, William. *Complete Poetry and Prose of William Blake, Newly Revised Edition*, ed. David V. Erdman. New York: Anchor Books/ Doubleday, 1988.

Buber, Martin. *I and Thou.* Trans. Walter Kaufman. New York: Simon and Schuster, 1970.

Couliano, Ioan P. *The Tree of Gnosis: Gnostic Mythology from Early Christianity to Modern Nihilism*. Trans. H.S. Wiesner and Ioan P. Couliano. San Francisco: HarperSanFrancisco, 1990.

Delany, Samuel R. "About Five Thousand One Hundred and Seventy Five Words." *Extrapolation* 10 (1969), 52-66.

Desjardins, Michel. "Retrofitting Gnosticism: Philip K. Dick and Christian Origins." In Tina Pippin and George Aichele, eds., *Violence, Utopia, and the Kingdom of God.* London and New York: Routledge, 1998, 122-133.

Dick, Philip K. *The Man in the High Castle*. New York: G.P. Putnam's Sons, 1962.

——. *The Three Stigmata of Palmer Eldritch*. 1965; rpt. New York: Vintage/Random House, 1991.

——. *Ubik.* 1969; rpt. New York: Vintage/Random House, 1991.

——. *Our Friends From Frolix 8.* New York: Ace Publishing Corporation, 1970.

——. *VALIS*. 1981; rpt. New York: Vintage/Random House, 1991.

——. *The Divine Invasion*. 1981; rpt. Vintage/Random House, 1991.

——. *The Transmigration of Timothy Archer.* 1982; rpt. New York: Vintage/Random House, 1991.

——. "The Mainstream that Through the Ghetto Flows: An Interview With Philip K. Dick." *Missouri Review* 7 no. 2 (Winter 1984), 164-185.

——. *Radio Free Albemuth.* 1985; rpt. New York: Vintage/Random House, 1998.

——. "Notes for work-in-progress, Circa August 1974." *The Philip K. Dick Society Newsletter* 9/10 (January 1986). Audio cassette.

——. *The Collected Stories of Philip K. Dick, Vol. 1*. New York: Citadel Twilight/Carol Publishing Group, 1987.

——. *In Pursuit of Valis: Selections From the Exegesis*, Lawrence Sutin, ed. Novato, California: Underwood-Miller, 1991.

——. *The Shifting Realities of Philip K. Dick: Selected Literary and Philosophical Writings,* ed. Lawrence Sutin. New York: Vintage/Random House, 1995.

——. *The Selected Letters of Philip K. Dick, Volume 3: 1974*, ed. Paul Williams. Novata, California: Underwood-Miller, 1991.

——. *The Selected Letters of Philip K. Dick, Volume 4: 1975-1976*, ed. Don Herron. Novata, California: Underwood-Miller, 1992.

——. *The Selected Letters of Philip K. Dick, Volume 5: 1977-1979*, ed. Don Herron. Novata, California: Underwood-Miller, 1993.

Dick, Tessa B. "Letter to The Philip K. Dick Society." *The Philip K. Dick Society Newsletter* 17 (April 1988), 12-13.

Disch, Thomas M. *The Dreams our Stuff is Made of: How Science Fiction Conquered the World*. New York: The Free Press, 1998.

WORKS CITED

DiTomasso, Lorenzo. "Gnosticism and Dualism in the Early Fiction of Philip K. Dick." *Science Fiction Studies* vol. 28 (Spring 2001), 49-65.

"Lorenzo DiTomasso on Rossi (Letter to *Extrapolation*)." *Extrapolation* 42 no. 1 (Spring 2001), 93-96.

Dumont, Jean-Noël. "Between Faith and Melancholy: Irony and the Gnostic Meaning of Dick's 'Divine Trilogy.'" *Science Fiction Studies* 45, July 1988. Reprinted in R.D. Mullen et. al., eds. *On Philip K. Dick: 40 Articles From Science-Fiction Studies.* Terre Haute and Greencastle, Indiana: SF-TH, Inc., 1992, 240-242.

Farmer, Philip José. *To Your Scattered Bodies Go*. New York: Berkely Medallion, 1971.

Fitting, Peter. "*Ubik*: The Deconstruction of Bourgeois SF." *Science Fiction Studies* 5, March 1975. Reprinted in R.D. Mullen et. al., eds. *On Philip K. Dick: 40 Articles From Science-Fiction Studies.* Terre Haute and Greencastle, Indiana: SF-TH, Inc., 1992, 41-49.

Galbreath, Robert. "Salvation-Knowledge: Ironic Gnosticism in *Valis* and *The Flight to Lucifer*." In Gary Wolfe, ed., *Science Fiction Dialogues*. Chicago: Academy Chicago, 1982, 115-132.

Gillespie, Bruce, ed., *Philip K. Dick: Electric Shepherd.* Melbourne, Australia: Norstrilia, 1975.

Hackett, Nancy, "Letter to The Philip K Dick Society." *The Philip K. Dick Society Newsletter* 16 (January 1988), 4 and 14.

Huxley, Aldous. *The Perennial Philosophy*. 1944; rpt. New York: Harper and Row, 1970.

Jonas, Hans. *The Gnostic Religion: The Message of the Alien God and the Beginnings of Christianity, Second Edition, revised*. Boston: Beacon Press, 1963, 1991.

Katz, Steven. "The 'Conservative' Character of Mystical Experience." In Katz, ed., *Mysticism and Religious Traditions*. New York: Oxford University Press, 1983, 3-60.

Ketterer, David. *New Worlds for Old: The Apocalyptic Imagination, Science Fiction, and American Literature*. Bloomington, Indiana: Indiana University Press, 1974.

Kinney, Jay. "Summary of the Exegesis Based on Preliminary Forays." *The Philip K. Dick Society Newsletter* 3 (1984), 1 and 13.

Lee, Gwen and Doris Elaine Sauter. *What If Our World Is Their Heaven? The Final Conversations of Philip K. Dick.* Woodstock and New York: The Overlook Press, 2000.

Luther, Martin. "Heidelberg Disputation." Trans. Harold J. Grimm. In *Luther's Works, vol. 31, ed. Harold J. Grimm and Helmut T. Lehmann. Philadelphia: Muhlenberg Press, 1957, 35-70.*

———. *"The Adoration of the Sacrament."* Trans. Abdel Ross Wentz. In *Luther's Works, vol. 36, ed. Abdel Ross Wentz and Helmut T. Lehmann. Philadelphia: Muhlenberg Press, 1957, 269-305.*

———. *"The Sacrament of the Body and Blood of Christ—Against the Fanatics."* Trans. Frederick C. Ahrens. In *Luther's Works, vol. 36, ed. Abdel Ross Wentz and Helmut T. Lehmann. Philadelphia: Muhlenberg Press, 1957, 329-361.*

McGrath, Alister. *Luther's Theology of the Cross.* Oxford: Basil Blackwell Inc., 1985.

Mullen, R.D. et. al., eds. *On Philip K. Dick: 40 Articles From Science-Fiction Studies.* Terre Haute and Greencastle, Indiana: SF-TH, Inc., 1992.

Platt, Charles. *Dream Makers: The Uncommon People Who Write Science Fiction.* New York: Berkley Books, 1980.

Reynolds, J. B. "The PKDS Interview With Tessa B. Dick (and Christopher Dick)." *The Philip K. Dick Society Newsletter* 13 (February 1987), 2-9.

Rickman, Gregg. *Philip K. Dick: The Last Testament.* Long Beach, California: Fragments West/Valentine Press, 1985.

———. *Philip K. Dick: In His Own Words.* Long Beach, CA: Fragments West/Valentine Press, 1984, 133.

Robinson, Kim Stanley. *The Novels of Philip K. Dick.* Ann Arbor, Michigan: UMI Research Press, 1984.

Rossi, Umberto. "Umberto Rossi on DiTomasso (Letter to *Extrapolation*)." *Extrapolation* 42 no. 1 (Spring 2001), 88-93.

Smart, Ninian. "Interpretation and Mystical Experience." In Richard Woods, ed., *Understanding Mysticism*. New York: Doubleday, 1980, 78-91.

Smith, Richard. "Afterword: The Modern Relevance of Gnosticism." In James M. Robinson, ed., *The Nag Hammadi Library in English, Third, Completely Revised Edition*. San Francisco: HarperSanFrancisco, 1988, 532-549.

Spinelli, Ernesto. "Philip K. Dick and the Philosophy of Uncertainty." *The Philip K. Dick Society Newsletter* 28 (March 1992), 19-22.

Spinrad, Norman. *Science Fiction in the Real World*. Carbondale, Illinois: Southern Illinois University Press, 1990.

Star, Alexander. "The God in the Trash." *New Republic* December 6, 1993: 34-42.

Sutin, Lawrence. *Divine Invasions: A Life of Philip K. Dick*. New York: Citadel Press/Carol Publishing Group, 1991.

Suvin, Darko. *Metamorphoses of Science Fiction: On the Poetics and History of a Literary Genre*. New Haven and London: Yale University Press, 1979.

Teilhard de Chardin, Pierre. *Toward the Future*. Trans. René Hague. New York: Harcourt Brace Jovanovich, 1975.

Tobin, Thomas H. "Logos," in David Noel Freedmen, ed.-in-chief, *The Anchor Bible Dictionary*, vol. 4, New York: Doubleday, 1992, 348-356.

Underhill, Evelyn. "The Essentials of Mysticism." In Richard Woods, ed., *Understanding Mysticism*. New York: Doubleday, 1980, 26-41.

Warrick, Patricia. "The Encounter of Taoism and Fascism in *The Man in the High Castle*." *Science Fiction Studies* 21, July 1980. Reprinted in R.D. Mullen et. al., eds. *On Philip K. Dick: 40 Articles From Science-Fiction Studies*. Terre Haute and Greencastle, Indiana: SF-TH, Inc., 1992, 74-90.

———. "Philip K. Dick's Answers to the Eternal Riddles." In Robert Reilly, ed., *The Transcendent Adventure: Studies of Religion in Science Fiction/Fantasy*. Westport, Connecticut: Greenwood Press, 1985, 108-126.

———. *Mind in Motion: The Fiction of Philip K. Dick*. Carbondale, Illinois: Southern Illinois University Press, 1987.

Williams, Michael Allen. *Rethinking "Gnosticism": An Argument for Dismantling a Dubious Category*. Princeton: Princeton University Press, 1996.

Williams, Paul. "Editor's note to 'An Excerpt From the Exegesis.'" *The Philip K. Dick Society Newsletter*, 12 (October 1986), 5.

——. *Only Apparently Real: The World of Philip K. Dick*. New York: Arbor House, 1986.

——, ed. *The Philip K. Dick Society Newsletter*. 30 issues (August 1983-December 1992).

Woodman, Tom. "Science fiction, religion and transcendence." In Patrick Parrinder, ed., *Science Fiction: A Critical Guide*. London: Longman Group, 1979, 110-130.

INDEX

Apostolides, Kleo, 74
Augustine of Hippo, St., 32, 37, 40, 42

Boucher, Anthony, 74
Buber, Martin, 17-19

Confessions of a Crap Artist, 74
Cosmic Puppets, The, 12

Delany, Samuel R., vi
Dick, Anne (neé Rubenstein), 74
Dick, Christopher Kenneth, 1, 5, 75
Dick, Isolde Freya, 75
Dick, Laura Archer, 74
Dick, Philip Kindred
    individual works: see separate headings.
    as cult leader, vii-viii
    2-3-74 experience of, 1-5, 13, 42, 45, 48, 50, 54-55, 71, 75
    philosophy in the early writing of, 12-22
    religious background, 13
    and Episcopal church, 14-15, 32, 63, 74-75
    and Marxism, 24-26
    and Gnosticism, 27-32, 43-44, 47, 49
    and Christianity, 13-15, 31-44, 54-55, 57-58, 62-67
    11-17-80 theophany of, 32-33, 48-52, 71
    drug use, 74, 75

Dick, Tessa (neé Busby), 1, 5, 14, 32, 75
Divine Invasion, The, 3, 11-12, 30, 38, 41, 52
Disch, Thomas M., vii
Dr. Bloodmoney, 73

Eucharist, see transubstantiation
Exegesis, viii, 5-10, 27, 29-30, 32-33, 34, 39-40, 43, 45-49, 51-52, 68, 70-71
    See also speculative theology
Eye in the Sky, 20

Farmer, Philip José, vi
Fitting, Peter, 24-26
Flow My Tears, the Policeman Said, 1

gnosticism, 27-32, 43-44, 47, 49

Hackett, Nancy 14, 75

I Ching see Taoism

Jeter, K.W., 10

logos, 37-44, 59, 68
Luther, Martin, 58-59, 63, 67

Man in the High Castle, The, 26-27, 38-39, 74
Morlin, Jeanette, 73-74
mystical experience, 78-71

Our Friends From Frolix 8, 34-35

Paul, Saint, 1, 12n, 16, 33-37, 53, 67
Penultimate Truth, The, 14
Philo of Alexandria, 40
Pike, James A., Bishop, 3
Plato, 22, 34, 40, 53, 55-56
Powers, Tim, 10

Radio Free Albemuth, 39n, 44, 45, 68
revelation, 54-56, 58-60
"Roog," 21, 74

Scanner Darkly, A, 12n, 36, 75
science fiction, *see* speculative fiction.
Simulacra, The, 14
Solar Lottery, The, 12, 74
speculative fiction,
    and religion, v-ix, 12-13
    and apocalyptic literature, vi-vii
    as popular genre, 23-24, 59, 65-67
speculative theology, viii-ix, 6, 46-53, 70-72
Spinrad, Norman, viii
Suvin, Darko, v

Taoism, 26-27, 29, 40
Teilhard de Chardin, Pierre, 61-62
theology of obscurity, 38-40, 56-68
Three Stigmata of Palmer Eldritch, The, 1, 15-20, 21, 62, 74-75
Transmigration of Timothy Archer, The, 10, 11-12, 35, 47
transubstantiation, 14, 16, 31, 61-65, 75

Ubik, 20-21, 24-26
VALIS, 10-11, 27, 28, 30n, 39n, 45, 47